PRAISE FOR MICHAEL COLGRASS'
ADVENTURES OF AN AMERICAN COMPOSER

"You've got to read ADVENTURES OF AN AMERICAN COMPOSER. If you have ever wondered what shenanigans can go on in the music business, in both jazz and classical, Michael Colgrass—a most gifted composer, free lance musician and all 'round percussionist—has done it all, has seen it all. He writes in a brilliant, breezy, no-nonsense style of the lowest to the loftiest connections. He tells it as it is in 89 delicious vignettes."

Gunther Schuller, *Composer, Conductor, Writer and Jazz Historian*

"Witty, personal and touching, Michael Colgrass has written a wonderful collection of thoughts and reminiscences. Those who know him and his music will be delighted, and those who do not will be highly entertained."

Leonard Slatkin, *Music Director, Detroit Symphony Orchestra; Principal Guest Conductor, Pittsburgh Symphony Orchestra*

"As seen in the likes of Camille Saint-Säens, Artie Shaw, Leonardo Acosta, Nicolas Slonimsky, Bill Crow and a few others, Michael Colgrass belongs to that elite group of musicians possessing the ability to communicate through the written word. But even fewer can speak fluently about Jazz, classical and other musical languages like Colgrass, all of it with so much wisdom, humanity and great sense of humor. I love this new book of his!"

Paquito D'Rivera, *Nine-time Grammy Award-winning jazz musician; author of "My Sax Life"*

"The spectrum of names is astonishing, from Louis Prima to John Coltrane to Aaron Copland to John Cage to Leonard Bernstein to Charles Munch and Dizzy Gillespie to Albert Einstein. It's a highly entertaining read but at the same time, it is quite essential reading for anyone who cares about music."

Larry Weinstein, *Director/Producer, Rhombus Media; 1986 Academy Award nominee; 1993 International Emmy Award winner*

"ADVENTURES OF AN AMERICAN COMPOSER reads like an intimate dinner party with Michael holding forth; impish, witty, a string of poignant vignettes detailing his unconventional and fascinating musical journey."

Janet Arms, *Assistant Principal Flutist, New York City Opera*

"...a compelling, insightful, and enormously entertaining read. Gaining insight into what has motivated and fed the creative process of Michael Colgrass throughout his distinguished career has been quite inspiring, as well as simply hilarious. This book is a must for any passionate music lover!"

Cynthia Phelps, *Principal Violist, New York Philharmonic*

"Through this collection of adventures Michael reveals that the source of true inspiration is a life filled with passion, curiosity and humanity. His stories are human, but the extraordinary results of his life's work make Michael an American treasure. Anyone who dreams should read and reflect upon the life lessons in this wonderful autobiography."

Allan McMurray, *Distinguished Professor, Robert and Judy Charles Professor of Conducting, Director of Bands, College of Music University of Colorado*

"Half of a musician's life is like a moth to the flame: we follow a calling to our path. The other half is utter chaos, a series of accidents, happy and otherwise, that get us where we're going. Michael Colgrass captures both, with intelligence, humor, and a warm heart."

Karl Paulnack, *Director, Music Division, The Boston Conservatory*

"Michael Colgrass is a storyteller. We experience a unique journey as he tells the best story of them all: his very own. Michael's fertile imagination, wit and tenacity allow a hugely informative and rewarding book to emerge. There is simply never a dull moment. One is grateful for the opportunity to learn from one of the world's most talented and colourful people."

Dame Evelyn Glennie DBE, *Percussion Soloist, Motivational Speaker*

"I loved these stories. It is exciting and gratifying when a composer possessed of such a strong, individual voice as Michael Colgrass, shares the evolution of his path as a music creator. His collection of anecdotes will be an inspiration, especially to those courageous young musicians who aspire to be composers."

Frances Richard, *Vice President and Director of Concert Music, American Society of Composers, Authors and Publishers (ASCAP)*

MICHAEL
COLGRASS

*Adventures of
an American Composer*

edited by Neal and Ulla Colgrass

Published by
Meredith Music Publications
a division of G.W. Music, Inc.
4899 Lerch Creek Ct., Galesville, MD 20765
http://www.meredithmusic.com

MEREDITH MUSIC PUBLICATIONS and its stylized double M logo
are trademarks of
MEREDITH MUSIC PUBLICATIONS, a division of G.W. Music, Inc.

Cover photo: Paul Hoeffler
Cover and text design: Shawn Girsberger

International Standard Book Number: 978-1-57463-155-5
Cataloging-in-Publication Data is on file with the Library of Congress.
Library of Congress Control Number: 2009932022
Printed and bound in U.S.A

CONTENTS

INTRODUCTION

WHILE PLAYING SOCCER WITH MY EIGHT-YEAR-OLD SON IN OUR living room, the ball flew past me into the net. "How's that possible?" I asked. "I was covering the whole net with my arms and legs."

He gave me a somber look and said, "Michael, there's a big difference between the way you see yourself and the way you really are." I looked to my wife for sympathy, but she was too busy laughing.

Thirty years later, when I felt the urge to write about my life, I thought about Neal's remark. If I don't know who I really am, how can I write an autobiography? So I decided to write about interesting episodes in my life instead—pivotal stories that readers can piece together to form a picture of me and the creative generation to which I belong.

Although my parents had no interest in music, I was irresistibly drawn to jazz at age 10 when I saw Ray Bauduc play the drums in a movie. Two years later I formed my first band, determined to be the world's greatest jazz drummer. I still cut up in grammar school music class and tormented my high school band director by knocking over a domino setup of percussion instruments. But outside school I was dead serious about developing as a musician.

I met major bandleaders of the swing era—Benny Goodman, Gene Krupa, Lionel Hampton and others who were charmed by pencil portraits I had drawn of them. I even disguised myself as an adult to slip into the Pershing Ballroom on Chicago's South Side to hear Charlie Parker, Max Roach and Ray Brown. Backstage at Chicago's Civic Opera House I witnessed a private memorial, where a mysterious figure—either Miles Davis or Kenny Dorham—played taps in the dark over the body of drummer Big Sid Catlett.

As my world grew, I became a freelance percussionist and composer in New York. I met John Cage, who showed me how to compose by shaking pepper on music paper; Henry Brant, who smiled when I told him to toss his music in the fire; Aaron Copland, who cornered me for an opinion on his first 12-tone orchestra piece; Dizzy Gillespie, whose magnetic head made a pendant twirl crazily; and Harry Partch, who likened breaking musical tradition to intimacy with a cow. I also had a hot-and-cold acquaintance with Leonard Bernstein and a surprise backstage encounter with Elizabeth Taylor. As a percussionist, I played under Stravinsky after he had sipped enough Chivas Regal whiskey to lose his way in the "Stravinsky conducts Stravinsky" recording of *The Rite of Spring*. I also played in the European premiere of Elliott Carter's *Double Concerto* under conductor Bruno Maderna, who—despite his apparent distaste for American musicians—waited nervously for me to signal him that the piece was ending.

What's more, music opened my life to other encounters—with a shaman in Bali, spies in Cold War Bucharest and Vopos police who removed me from a train at gunpoint in East Germany.

All this added up to a career in music, but my dream of writing music for a living came later. I had no idea that such a thing was considered almost impossible. People ask how I did it and I don't know what to tell them. But a practice of Walt Disney's comes to mind. He was said to have three rooms for his cartoonists and animators: the Dreaming Room, the Realists' Room, and the Critics' Room. First they all went into the Dreaming Room. Here all dreams were encouraged, no matter how wild. Next was the Realists' Room, where no dreams were allowed. Instead they asked, "How much will it cost?" "How many people do we need?" "How long will it take?" Then to the Critics' Room: "Is it worth doing?" "Is someone else doing it better?" "Are we good enough?" When they returned to the Dreaming Room, they knew *how* to make the dream work.

This triple perspective describes the three spaces of my mind—in life and in composing. When I write music, the Dreamer goes wild with a new passage. Then my Realist tells me it's too high for the French horns, so I lower it. Then my Critic might remind me that I wrote a similar passage in my last piece, so I adjust it. This triumvirate makes it possible for me to create, and I rarely get stuck, because composing for me is a *group* process of three partners.

My Dreamer-Realist-Critic has helped me ever since I started running Three Jacks and Jill, my first band in grade 8. But I needed help from people to learn the disciplines and skills of a musician: my father taught me how to memorize; Don Coy, jazz lover, guided me as a listener; Paul Price, my percussion teacher at the University of Illinois, challenged me to write music and played everything I wrote; Gene Weigel and Ben Weber taught me how to compose. Bill Hickey and Jerzy Grotowski later showed me theater skills, and John Grinder opened me to the world of Neuro-Linguistic Programming. Most of all my wife, Ulla, encouraged me every step of the way.

Joseph Campbell, in his book *The Hero with a Thousand Faces*, describes the hero's journey: responding to a call, crossing a threshold, acquiring a guardian and venturing into the unknown, where you encounter demons who become enemies or allies depending on how you relate to them. Then you return to tell the tale.

My life has been a series of threshold crossings, and these stories are my tales. ❧

PART I
1942–1949

RECIPE FOR
MY CONCEPTION

I WAS CONCEIVED ON THE KITCHEN FLOOR OF A BROWN BRICK
bungalow in Brookfield, Illinois, in the summer of 1931. My mother was
desperately trying to have a boy, because she'd given birth to a girl six
years before and earned the wrath of my Italian grandma: a *paesan* would
have known to have a boy first, for the good of the family, Grandma
said. But Mom was Irish and didn't know. Everyone on my father's side
was 25 years off the boat from a grape-growing village in southern Italy
and was anxious to see a first male Colagrossi born in America.

Seeking guidance, my mother turned to her best friend and
neighbor, Amber Bebinger—a large, freckled woman with the spirit
of a teenager and a body that shook like Jell-O when she laughed.
Mom believed Amber had gained psychic powers by reading books
on ESP and reincarnation. Did she know how to make sure her second child would be a boy? Certainly, Amber said: abstain from sex
for all but one selected day in the month and she would have a boy
exactly nine months later. Where Amber found this formula nobody
knows, but Mom took it as psychic revelation.

The chosen day was July 22nd at 10 p.m. A heat wave was stifling
central Illinois, so my parents slept on the kitchen floor with doors

and windows open for air circulation. Nine months later—on April 22nd, 1932—she told the doctor she was going to have her baby that very day. He doubted it because she had no labor pains, but she insisted and was taken to the hospital. At 10:20 p.m., I was born without giving her a single labor pain.

Grandma was euphoric, and even my six-year-old sister Gloria liked her new baby brother, who was nicknamed Buddy. My second sister, Catherine, was born 14 years later.

I don't know if arriving exactly nine months after my conception in a kitchen had any effect on me, but I am still punctual and I do love to eat, especially pasta—which I always have *al dente* in honor of my father's virile efforts on my behalf. ❋

"I'M A DRUMMER!"

My musical birth came at age 10 when I saw Dixieland jazz musicians Ray Bauduc and Bobby Haggart play "Big Noise from Winnetka" in the movie *Reveille with Beverly*.

My parents often walked me and my sister to the Strand, a tiny movie house that provided Brookfield's culture—James Cagney thrillers and Hopalong Cassidy westerns and the taste of buttered popcorn. But on this night my eyes were fogging over until Bob Crosby & the Bobcats hit the screen. Smart in black tie and white jackets, they wailed away on saxes and trombones against a glittering city skyline.

The camera panned to Bauduc on drums and Haggart on bass. Bauduc's sticks flashed in a blur, clicking and tapping on drums and cowbells and wood blocks—*tink-a-boom tok-tink-a-toom-toom tink-a-tock*—candy to my ears. Haggart's quick fingering on the bass strings—*doom-doom-ba-doom-doom*—blended invisibly with the tom-toms while he whistled the tune. These wizards spoke a language that seemed designed especially for me. As my joy peaked, Bauduc turned and tapped his sticks on the bass strings while Haggart fingered the pitches. I almost floated toward the screen.

I was in a daze for the rest of the movie. Walking out of the theater, I begged my father to buy me a drum. He said I would first have to learn to care for expensive things, and reminded me of my bike, which was still rusty from the night I left it out in the rain.

"But I would never leave a drum out in the rain," I said.

If I really wanted a drum, he said, I'd have to prove it by saving money. How could I? I was only 10 years old! Then I remembered that some of the older boys made money in the summer as golf caddies. So I biked over to the LaGrange Country Club that weekend and charmed the manager into hiring me as a Green Badge caddy. I earned $1.80 a day, lugging 36 holes for 10 weeks, and worked my way up to an Orange Badge for $2.20 a day. This was before the age of golf carts, so I had to hoist one or two bags on my shoulders on long, boiling-hot treks across the course. At the end of the day, I skinny-dipped in the water holes to rescue lost balls to sell.

By September, I'd saved $29. My father and I went hunting for a snare drum at Frank's Drum Shop in Chicago, where I ran around tapping on every drum I saw. The wooden and metal shells and calfskin drumheads smelled beautiful. I finally settled on a snare drum with a silvery shell that sounded a lot like Bauduc's. It cost $31, plus tax. My father pulled me aside and said, "I'll make you a deal: I'll pay half and you pay half, and we'll put the rest in the bank"—my first lesson in economics.

When I got the drum home, I tried to play the syncopated rhythms Bauduc played on-screen. I had only one drum of course, and Bauduc had a whole set, but I made up for it by tapping on everything in the house that didn't move. From that point on, everything I did felt like the first time. "This is the first time I've been in school since I'm a drummer." "The first time I've seen a movie since I'm a drummer." "The first time I've been swimming since I'm a drummer." Life was starting all over again. ❧

THREE JACKS AND A JILL

I PAID FOR MORE DRUMS BY SETTING PINS IN A BOWLING ALLEY, AND put together a band called Three Jacks and a Jill. The Jill was an accordionist in school named Jarmela, whom I secretly loved. Every time she squeezed the accordion, her red hair swished back and forth and I imagined she was squeezing me. The Jacks were me and two guys on trumpet and piano. They could all read music, but I only read rhythms, so I would direct them by ear on popular dance tunes like "Tangerine," "Liza" and "It Had to be You"—all in a swing style without vocals. We rehearsed at my place because my drums were there and my family had an upright piano. I would tell them who should solo when and for how long. Of course, I got a lot of solos, being the arranger.

When I was 12, our band was playing for school basketball games and pep assemblies, and soon moved on to adult gigs at the Business-man's Association of Brookfield and the Kiwanis Club. Before I knew it, I was booking the group, negotiating fees, setting up schedules and making sure everyone knew where to go and when to be there. Sometimes I had to chase people down for rehearsal—like Warren, who would rather catch fly balls on the baseball field.

I also began getting the attention—and criticism—of adults. Between sets at a public dance in a park, the editor of the daily

Brookfield Enterprise took me aside and told me our "jazzy music" was too fast for older folks, who liked dancing to waltzes and polkas. "You're going to have to learn to give the public what it wants," he said. He was right in a way—I did emphasize virtuosity and made the playing more important than the dancing.

This was my first run-in with the problem that big dance bands of the day, like Tommy Dorsey's and Woody Herman's, would face in the '50s as swing gradually morphed into virtuosic bebop—great for the ear, but not designed for dancing. The bands that survived this transition, like Lawrence Welk's, stuck with the conservative '40s ballroom style, which was quiet, danceable and all background.

Stung by the editor's remark, I consoled myself thinking about our fans. At least *they* loved us—but they were our classmates. Now we were playing for a wider public and a broader spectrum of tastes. The editor struck a nerve because he had a point: I cared more about my music than the "consumer." I swore never to read the *Enterprise* again and felt a crack open between the artist's creative world and the public's commercial demands, a division that would only grow for me as a jazz musician and later as a composer—where I was often asked, "Who do you make music for—yourself or the public?" At 12, I had no idea what I was up against. ❋

SPITBALL SYMPHONY

"MICHAEL HASN'T PASSED A MUSIC TEST YET." I CONSIDERED THAT note scrawled on my fourth grade report card at S.E. Gross Elementary School to be a badge of honor. Boring scales and eye-glazing words like "chords" and "clefs" were foreign and incomprehensible to me, and the fact that we sang occasionally didn't help because no one taught us how—so it always sounded dreadful. Our teacher would make things worse by playing some stuffy symphonic music and saying things like, "This part represents a storm," and "This is like birds singing."

Fifth grade was no better. "If Michael would stop fooling around and disturbing others in music class he might accomplish something." I didn't stop to think what Miss McCann meant by that because I was too busy fooling around. I do remember a girl named Geraldine, who sat beside me in class. I would break her pencils and place the pieces back on her desk when she wasn't looking. One day she caught me and stabbed me in the palm with a newly sharpened pencil. I stopped breaking her pencils after that. But the lead mark, still on my hand, was another badge of honor—a battle scar to prove I survived Miss McCann's music class.

In seventh grade, my interim report card read, "All play and no work seems to be Michael's formula for no progress in music class."

In fact I had made a lot of progress in music class. I'd devised a system for sticking spitballs to the ceiling and competed with friends to see who could get the biggest collection above his seat. I was the undisputed champ at snapping these saliva-dampened little paper pellets with a ruler off the edge of my desk.

Everyone in class knew about it except Miss Nieman, until one day she turned from the board and saw me tearing paper into small pieces of ammunition. I kept still as her eyes moved slowly up to the ceiling and gazed at my hardened spit-wads. Miss Nieman looked at me quizzically and asked, "How did you do it?" Taken aback, I explained the whole process to her step by step while she nodded and the other kids listened. Then she simply returned to her blackboard full of musical leger lines, and the drone of clefs and chords continued.

When I walked into music class the next day, the ceiling was clean and I began paying attention for the first time. This was a memorable lesson in the value of rapport: if her face had split down the middle with rage, I would have devised some other torture for her, but she won me over by accepting my spitballs as an accomplishment. I felt obligated to be a good boy, especially being reseated in the front row.

Yet as the year droned on, I still didn't learn a thing about music. ✳

Waiting for the Caboose

I BOLDLY SIGNED UP FOR A REGIONAL SNARE DRUM CONTEST IN grade 6, but my confidence buckled when my band director, Mr. Wilkins, told me I would have to memorize a military drum solo out of a book. I could barely read the music, let alone memorize it. But I wanted to show off my skills to the world, so I presented my father with the dilemma. After all, fathers were supposed to know everything.

He was sitting in his favorite easy chair, smoking a pipe with Edgeworth tobacco, which smelled like leaves burning—a fragrance I loved. He looked surprised by my problem and pled ignorance, reminding me he couldn't read music or play drums himself. I still begged him to try.

He put down his pipe and opened the music book on the ottoman for both of us to see. Though he couldn't read the notes, he noticed that the rhythms made shapes on the page, one after the other. "The music looks something like a train with cars on it," he said. He was right. It reminded me of the train to Chicago, which rolled through our town, often leaving us stuck in our car for long stretches while I counted passing train cars.

Moving his finger along the blocks of notes, he said, "Maybe the first thing you play could be the engine, the second the coal car, the third the oil car, then the freight car and the cattle car." That made sense to me. But then what? "Well, when you get to the caboose you know you're finished."

That painted a clear picture in my mind. With Mr. Wilkins' help, I started reading the music and visualizing my little solo as a long train—like the freight cars that rumbled across Grand Boulevard. In fact, my little fantasy train made reading music easier and more fun. I could just watch the cars going by and hear my rhythms as if they were wheels clacking along the tracks.

On the day of the contest, I lugged my sticks into our local public meeting hall crowded with kids. Some had even brought their own snare drums and I began to feel naked without one. Those kids looked so confident. What if I forgot everything I had memorized when I got up to play? One by one, each student played a solo on stage and sounded so good. I considered telling Mr. Wilkins I'd changed my mind. When my name was called, I walked up onto the stage, my heart pounding, and eyed row upon row of tense parents. Then a new feeling hit me—that this was my chance to show them what I could do. I looked at the drum, squeezed the sticks in my hand, heard the opening bar of my solo in my mind and before I knew it, I was rattling off my train, getting better with each stroke. I didn't want it to end.

When someone pinned a blue ribbon on my chest, I realized I was unimpressed by winning. What struck me was how good it felt to play for people, and how I could do it with such comfort and ease.

I think my confidence came from the way I'd learned the piece. The technique of breaking it down into little components would stick with me through my career as a percussionist, when I often had to learn music on the spot.

I have my father's train to thank for that. ✻

THE MOB INVITES
MY FATHER

"How did you become a composer?" That's a question I often hear, usually in conversation at a party. People assume I had musical parents, came from an artistic household or had honed my craft in special schools.

It was none of the above. Aside from my sister's piano lessons, music rarely entered my family home—except for the occasional pop songs of singers like Bing Crosby and the Andrews Sisters.

In our modest home at the corner of Grant and Madison, my mother was a homemaker and my father a former pro boxer. In fact, a peek into his history says more about my attitude toward career development than anything I learned in school.

Dad grew up on Chicago's West Side in a tough neighborhood called "The Patch," where he had to fight just to carry home a loaf of bread. At 5-foot-2, he was vulnerable to attacks, so he took up boxing. Soon he was competing in amateur contests and won the 1921 Midwest Golden Gloves Championship in the bantamweight division. Given the chance to go professional, he turned it down. When I later asked him why, he just said, "Boxers are bums."

But Chicago's infamous Forty-Two Gang didn't consider him a bum. A gang of hoodlums bent on hold-ups, rapes and murders, they wanted a pugilist like Dad on the payroll—anything to help them grab the attention of bootlegging gangs like Al Capone's. And Dad didn't dare turn them down. He didn't want to end up like the horses whose legs the Forty-Two Gang members hacked off to sell to horsemeat outlets. These weren't the kind of people he wanted to cross.

So he turned pro, as "Fightin' Jack Colgrass", a move that gang members respected. It gave him an excuse not to run night jobs, like robbing stores or threatening club owners, because everyone knew boxers went to bed early and got up before dawn to work out. My uncle once told me, "If anybody saw your father out on the street after 9:30 they would say to him"—here he assumed a gruff voice—"'Hey Jack, git home. Ya gotta train.'"

Dad was undefeated in the ring, but retired within a few years to avoid a costly nose operation that could have restricted his breathing for life. He wanted out of Chicago and the boxing business anyway, so he spent his savings on night school and learned drafting, which led to a job at the Imperial Brass Company on Chicago's West Side. He soon ran for a local Democratic committee seat and won, and was later appointed postmaster of Brookfield, where he served for 38 years.

Looking at this quiet and gentle man, you would never guess his background. He didn't like to talk about it either. The goal of an Italian immigrant in those days was to erase any trace of his heritage and become an American. When his fight manager told him, "You can't fight in the ring with a name like Colagrossi," he was only too happy to change it to Colgrass.

My father (whose real name was Michael) said little about his early years, but one day I cornered him with questions. He admitted very little, but said he'd taught and sparred with another Italian immigrant who also changed his name: Vincenzo Antonio Gibaldi, who became "Battling Jack McGurn" to get the bookings of an Irish boxer. As one of Capone's top enforcers, McGurn was also known as "Machine Gun Jack McGurn"—and reputedly helped plan and carry out the St. Valentine's Day Massacre.

When I told my father about McGurn's role in the gangland murder, he waved a hand and said, "Oh, I don't think Jack would do anything like that. In sparring practice he never took any cheap shots." I told him that McGurn took other shots that were very costly for some people!

Looking back, I wonder if my father's fighting genes gave me the extra oomph to persevere as a composer—to live for years on a low income and endure long stretches without performances. "We should get an award just for surviving," a composer once told me. My father certainly was a survivor.

So, was there culture in my family? Yes, there was—a culture of survival that's very different from Mozart's or Beethoven's, but a culture of which I'm very proud. ✳

TORMENTING
MY BAND TEACHER

As you may have guessed from my elementary school antics, I was not the ideal student. I carried on this tradition at Riverside-Brookfield High School, even though it had a band to keep me occupied. What I hated was our repertoire: mostly marches on the football field, and no jazz.

The end of football season brought no relief, because we launched into rehearsals of terrible cookie-cutter stuff that publishers sent to band directors with snappy titles like "Apples and Oranges," "Saturday in the Park" and "Cowboy Holiday"—which the whole band played in unison and usually out of tune. Or we lurched into transcriptions of obscure classical overtures that substituted a flock of clarinets for violins, and saxophones and euphoniums for cellos. Whenever anyone complained, Mr. Newmark, our stalwart band director, said we weren't good enough to play anything else. Small of stature and always irritable, Mr. Newmark was right to criticize our playing, but we all knew he couldn't make us any better either. For 45 minutes of band rehearsal, he spent more time pursing his lips in disgust than suggesting anything constructive.

He also made fun of us "drummers" who "can't read music," and claimed he could count on us to drop a drumstick or knock over a cymbal in the middle of a performance.

One day, determined to fulfill his belief in our incompetence, I set up every percussion instrument in the room to come crashing down at once. I showed up early for rehearsal and balanced my set of musical dominos, making sure one nudge would trigger a deafening crescendo of instruments as they fell to the floor.

With about 10 minutes left in rehearsal, I grew nervous about it—and was about to abandon the whole thing when Mr. Newmark began lecturing us on the value of discipline. That was all I needed. While he sermonized, I moved slowly toward the snare drum and, keeping my eyes on Mr. Newmark, pushed my little finger against the rim. The drum's weight shifted over onto two tom-toms and a field drum, which upset a tray stand of cowbells, wood blocks, triangles and cymbals. They landed on the precariously poised bass drum, which sent everything booming, clattering, banging and tinkling across the floor.

When the last cymbal finally stopped spinning, a few of my classmates giggled, but Mr. Newmark just stared. "Why don't you throw all the sticks out the window too?" he said. Well, he was the boss, so we heaved out every mallet and beater we had. Just below the window was the airshaft to the school incinerator, which silently swallowed up the sticks into infinity.

At that moment the bell rang. We all scooped up our books and vanished in multiple directions as Mr. Newmark, his lips pursed, stared coldly into the distance.

My noisy protest was just before Christmas, so by the time we dragged ourselves back in January, Mr. Newmark seemed to have forgotten all about it. Or maybe he hadn't. He was inexplicably nicer and even handed out a piece to feature me as jazz soloist on the drums. Miraculously, we developed a degree of mutual respect.

He talked less in rehearsals and instructed more, and I earned a good grade at the end of the year, though he did add an enigmatic remark: "Michael made a memorable contribution to band, and I wish him well in whichever direction he chooses to go away from here." ❧

MY PORTRAITS OF
JAZZ GREATS

IN HIGH SCHOOL I DREAMED OF HITTING THE ROAD WITH A GREAT
swing band, but dropping out at age 14 seemed wrong. Staying in
school was even worse—a gray-halled prison that taught me less
than I had learned playing in Three Jacks and a Jill. I longed to play
for a master musician like Benny Goodman or Tommy Dorsey, but
they didn't know me from the newspaper boy. Meeting them seemed
pure fantasy.

Then something happened: I sketched a picture of President
Roosevelt off the front page of the newspaper. I had a natural talent for drawing, which I had taken for granted while doodling whatever fascinated me—a human body, a map of the world, cartoon
faces of teachers—anything that distracted me from the dreariness
of school. But when I drew Roosevelt, my parents mentioned it to
everyone who came to the house. One day my father asked me to
make a portrait of my grandfather for my grandmother's birthday.
On the big day, everybody in our extended Italian family piled in for
the unveiling of my masterpiece. As uncles tussled my hair and their
wives air-kissed my cheeks, it struck me that I could put my drawing
skills to a more musical purpose.

Every week I saw ads in the paper for bands playing stage shows at the Oriental Theater in downtown Chicago, about a half-hour's ride from Brookfield. Long lines of autograph-seekers would form at the stage door, even during Illinois' bleak winters. I wondered if I could sketch my way right through the madding crowd.

My first attempt was trumpeter Charlie Spivak. I'd heard his band on the radio and knew he had a great drummer named Alvin Stoller. So I drew an 20" × 16" picture of Spivak using a new art pencil called Flamingo, which was softer and darker and made it easier to create dramatic contrasts.

I rode the streetcar to Cicero, where I connected to the elevated train to Chicago's loop and walked two blocks to the Oriental. The theater's carpeted halls and high ceilings seemed like a Greek palace to me. Would I really be hearing Spivak live? After an opening movie, the screen rose and colored lights shimmered on a curtain. Still unseen, the band began to play. My heart thumped against my ribs as the curtain pulled away and the band rolled out on a moving stage, the musicians basking in colored spotlights. I doubt I blinked once during the entire show.

Floating out the front door, I noticed a line of autograph-seekers forming around the corner on Dearborn Street, and my heart sank. It would take forever to get to the stage door.

So I went around the line to the stage door and showed my Spivak portrait to the one-eyed doorman. He nodded and said, "C'mon in, kid." Spivak was standing just inside the door to sign autographs. A jovial man with a red face and a flower in his lapel, he unrolled my picture and smiled. He asked if he could keep it. I was ecstatic. How far could I go with this?

Next was Benny Goodman (along with his bassist Slam Stewart and trumpeter Cootie Williams), then Jimmy Dorsey (and his drummer Karl Kiffe), Lionel Hampton, Buddy Rich and Woody Herman. My skills increased with every drawing. And I was getting to know

Mike, the one-eyed doorman, who introduced me to bandleaders without any questions. Each was impressed with his portrait and asked me about myself. I said I wanted to leave high school and go on the road as a featured child drummer. Most of them seemed impressed by my outspoken ambition, but they said I was too young to replace their special featured acts—singers, dancers or the occasional child prodigy booked by agents in New York or Hollywood. To me, those cities were the Land of Oz, and I was nowhere near the yellow brick road. ✳

SNEAKING IN
TO SEE GENE KRUPA

MY FIRST BIG DRUMMING IDOL WAS GENE KRUPA—THE HEIFETZ OF the drums and a household name. He was a star drummer in movies and his records sold everywhere. I copied his way of playing, even his way of combing his hair—straight back, with no part on the side. I was dying to talk to him and had a hundred questions. Just to get close to him would be a moment to remember. He was going to appear at the Panther Room of the Sherman Hotel, just a few blocks from the Oriental Theater, so I made him my next project.

But how could I, a 14-year-old kid, get close to him in a supper club?

Throughout these years of meeting bandleaders I had developed considerable confidence at getting into places kids couldn't go—like the Panther Room. So I drew an especially good portrait of Krupa with his shadow large on the back wall while he hovered over the drums. I wrapped it up in celluloid to keep it clean and took the streetcar and "L" into Chicago's loop. My standard budget for the trip included twenty-one cents for three Hershey bars, my food for the day.

I entered the Sherman Hotel and down the staircase to the supper club, where I slipped in with a cluster of people. It was about 6:30 p.m. But how would I find Krupa? There was no backstage door. Then I noticed musicians coming onto the bandstand through the kitchen off stage right. Acting like I belonged, I walked over to the kitchen's swinging doors and waited for someone to come through. Soon a waiter backed out balancing a large tray and I slipped in with the rhythm of the swinging doors. Ducking behind a partition by the dishwashers, I peeked out at the bustling kitchen and waited for Krupa. How long could I stand here without being discovered? The floor manager kept leaning in to tell the cooks to hurry, his elbow hovering right beside me—but he was too busy to notice a fidgety teenage trespasser. If I could just see Krupa in person, I would at least have that memory.

Finally Krupa walked in, flanked by two other musicians. He was shorter than I expected—from the movies I thought he was a giant. His dark wavy hair was combed back in a thick pompadour. I couldn't believe it. I was standing within a few feet of the world's greatest drummer! He was passing through quickly on his way to the stage, so I jumped out and told him my name. "I draw pictures of all the great musicians," I said. He looked at the picture, told me it was very good, smiled, and at my request signed it. Just then the head-waiter came through the doors. "Hey kid, how did you get in here?" He promptly escorted me through the supper club and into the Sherman Hotel lobby. I was deeply frustrated. In another moment I might have been able to arrange a date to talk with Krupa. But I controlled my feelings until I left the hotel.

I had to find someplace to be alone, so I went into the alley behind the hotel and sat on an orange crate amidst the garbage and let my emotions pour out. I must have cried for 10 minutes as I told the garbage cans around me all the things I had wanted to say to Krupa—that I was a drummer too, that I'd memorized all his solos from recordings, that I wanted to be like him because he was the most exciting musician I'd ever heard. Then I wiped my eyes, walked to the elevated train on Wabash, and went home. I never told my parents what happened.

"Some Kind of Genius"

As it turned out, I met Krupa again 26 years later when he played with his trio at the Metropole on Broadway. He was well past his public glory, and I was gaining my small share of recognition, having recently soloed in the premiere of my *Rhapsodic Fantasy for 15 Tuned Drums and Orchestra* with the Danish Radio Orchestra at Tivoli Gardens in Copenhagen. MCA Music in New York had just published the score. I thought Krupa might want to see it, especially because he'd had an idea for a similar drum to those designed for my piece—tunable tom-toms, designed and built for me by the former Chicago Symphony percussionist Al Payson.

So I heard Krupa play on a Saturday matinee with my score in hand. At 63, he sounded as good as ever. When he took a break, I walked up and introduced myself, offering to show him my latest piece for multiple drums and orchestra. He invited me to his dressing room and we sat down. His hair was streaked with gray and his face, now fuller, marked with age lines.

My concerto was rhythmically complex. I had devised my own notation for a technique called "metrical modulation," a special treatment of rhythm and tempo created by Elliott Carter. Most music is written in common meters like four-four, two-four and six-eight, but my notation showed meters in odd fractions, like three-five, four-three and eight-twenty-five—a new way of showing these rhythms. Instead of being round, the note heads were square, rectangular, triangular and star-shaped. The way his eyes strayed randomly over the page told me he was not used to looking at symphonic scores, let alone my new meters. As I explained the rhythms, he nodded, occasionally frowning, like he was searching for a way to relate this to his own music. Just then Anita O'Day walked in and Krupa said, "Say hello to Michael, he's some kind of genius."

I felt a stab in my stomach. I realized I had alienated myself from him by speaking a language he didn't understand. When I suggested that we get together to talk more about percussion music, he said, "Thanks, but I'm very jealous of the little free time I have."

My first attempt to get to know him was thwarted because I was too young, and the second because I was too "advanced." I had shed many musical skins since my days of imitating Krupa's dramatic tom-tom solos. Yet he had been one of the main inspirations to me as a youngster, and I should have let him know. The mistakes we make! ✳

GETTING
GERTIE'S GARTER

MY MOST AMBITIOUS DRAWING WAS A NEAR-LIFE-SIZE PORTRAIT OF Cab Calloway. It caught him in his famous "Hi-di-hi-di-ho" pose, leaning back with a broad smile, eyes heavenward, in fancy tux and tails, waving a baton and singing his heart out.

The Panther Room of Chicago's Sherman Hotel was featuring his band that week. I snuck up the back stairs of the hotel and knocked on room 800, where all the bandleaders stayed. Calloway opened the door himself. Dressed in his famous tux with the super-wide lapels, he gave me a smile. He was just getting ready to go downstairs for his Saturday matinee performance. I could see he was good natured and liked kids, which gave me the confidence to tell him how I drew all the big band leaders who came to Chicago. I unrolled my giant drawing and handed it to him.

He looked at it, then me, then back again. *"You* drew this?" We talked for only a few minutes, but I told him about Three Jacks and a Jill and my dream of being a professional drummer. He nodded knowingly, as if he remembered dreaming the same dream at my age. He ran his fingers over my drawing admiringly and refused to take it as a gift, saying I would someday wish I'd kept it.

Walking back to Wabash Street for the elevated train, I basked in my encounter with one of the big band jazz icons. But little did I know that another special meeting was right around the corner.

As I walked toward the Oriental Theater I noticed big black plastic letters on the marquee: "Marie (The Body) MacDonald"! She had gorgeous blue eyes, silky straw-colored hair and all the curves a 14-year-old boy could fantasize about. The poster described her as an up-and-coming star promoting her new movie *Getting Gertie's Garter*.

So I went around to the stage door and gave doorman Mike my usual greeting as I opened the door.

"Hi, Mike."

"Hi, Mike," he said. "You wanna meet Marie?" She was just coming down the stairs, glittering jewelry and a silver-sequined gown radiating light all around her. Her heels and beehive hairdo gave her an almost magisterial look.

"Miss MacDonald," Mike said, "this kid draws pictures of all the celebrities who come through here." She saw the large roll tucked under my arm and asked if that was one of them. I unrolled Calloway's picture.

"You *drew* that?"

I beamed.

"Would you do one of me?" She turned to a tense man behind her and asked him for a publicity shot. He curtly said they were all given out at autograph signings. "Then go get one from the showcase out front." Scowling like I was something he'd just stepped on, he grabbed the window keys from Mike and jerked his thumb for me to follow.

I purposely took my time at the showcase windows. "C'mon kid," he growled. I slowly nodded at one of Miss MacDonald's glossies, and he stepped up with the key. Then I turned to another. "Or maybe this one." When I thought he was about to detonate I finally chose one, thanked him and walked to the elevated train.

Back home, I struggled to get her down on paper. Her airbrushed photo showed none of the facial contours or character she revealed in life. When I returned to the Oriental Theater six months later for her return tour, Mike phoned upstairs and gave me the okay. I found her in her dressing room at a mirror rimmed with naked bulbs. Two of the lights were burned out and the place smelled musty. The front of the theater may have resembled a palace, but backstage seemed suited to storage.

She looked relaxed without makeup, unlike the first time I met her. Her voice was soft and conveyed the feeling that we had all the time in the world. Unwrapping my drawing, I admitted I'd had trouble with it; I was afraid I didn't show her at her best. She cracked a smile, looked at me with a tip of her head and said, "On the contrary, you make me look too good."

She gestured to a couch beside her and asked me about myself as she went back to her makeup. Her little nods seemed to show genuine interest in the stories about my band and my ambitions. I think she found it easier to show her human side to a youngster and not worry about playing the glamorous star.

"You're going to go far in this world," she said, "because you're very assertive."

I asked what that word meant.

"When you want something, you go after it."

"Well, doesn't everybody?"

She stopped in mid-motion, glanced at me and took a long look at herself in the mirror. "No…they don't."

Twenty years later, I read in the paper that she had died from an overdose of pills—after seven marriages and several nervous breakdowns.

Visiting my childhood home in Brookfield many years later, I was surprised to discover my drawing of her in the attic. For the first time I noticed how sad her eyes looked. Had I actually captured that?

I recalled how her gaze had lost itself in my drawing when I first showed it to her. I wondered if she was pleased, or maybe saddened, to see her real self revealed by a teenage boy.

I'm sure many men have fantasized about her as a woman, but my fantasy is to return and tell her that I remember her humanity. ✳

LAST STOP:
LOUIS PRIMA

LOUIS PRIMA CHANGED MY MIND ABOUT QUITTING SCHOOL AND hitting the road with a jazz band.

Carrying a portrait of the bandleader, I approached him backstage one day at the Oriental Theater. He greeted me like an old friend with that warm, smoky voice of his, and invited me to his dressing room to meet his mother. Angelina was a small, round woman in black with a robust smile.

She let out a cry when I unrolled my drawing. "Oh, you must draw another one for me!" When I told her my father was Italian, she clapped her hands. "Of course! Such talent!" Spurred by her questions, I told her about my Italian family while Prima busied himself around the dressing room. She said her son was coming back to Chicago in a few months, a perfect time for me to return with another picture.

I left, excited at the prospect of pleasing both Prima and his mother. They had made me feel so welcome. I made a drawing not only for Prima's mother, but another for his drummer, Jimmy Vincent, and singer, Judy Lynn.

When I knocked on Prima's dressing room door in the spring and showed him my new pictures, he was delighted and sat me down to ask about my aspirations. I repeated what I'd said to all the other bandleaders: I wanted to leave school and play professionally. He gave his nose a big rub before answering. "I'll tell you what I'll do," he said. "I never finished high school and I am very sorry about that. You finish school and when you graduate, come back and play for me, and if you can play any music I put in front of you, I'll give you the job in my band."

For the first time I felt like someone had taken me seriously as a fellow musician. I stopped drawing portraits of bandleaders and became a better student. Finishing high school, I went on to study music at the university and expand my musical horizons with classical music, playing and composing. All other memories seemed to fade.

Years later, when I realized the influence of Prima's words, he was already gone, having died in 1978 after a brain tumor operation. I've often fantasized about conversations with him, telling him of my musical accomplishments since we last talked. I imagine inviting him to a premiere and handing him a signed, published score, with thanks for being kind to a kid he hardly knew. ❋

THE SPAGHETTI DID IT!

I SPENT MY TEENAGE YEARS POUNDING AWAY ON DRUMS IN THE basement to the sound of jazz recordings. Always improvising, I'd never bothered to develop my music-reading skills or to appreciate classical music, which was never within earshot anyway.

One day I was playing along with a Count Basie record when the lights blinked on and off—my mother's attempt to cut through the din. She was yelling something about a call from the West Suburban Symphony Orchestra. When I picked up the phone, a man said they were desperate (obviously, if they called *me*) for a sub at rehearsal tonight.

A violinist in the orchestra picked me up. On the way to rehearsal I confessed to my lack of classical music experience and she said, "Don't worry, the conductor will cue you. He's very good—he's the conductor of the Chicago Civic." That was supposed to reassure me, but it made me all the more nervous. The Chicago Civic what? It sounded so scholarly, so distant from my experience.

I walked into the rehearsal with drumsticks in hand and met the timpanist, the only other percussionist that night. He was a stuffy old guy who looked at me like I had just crawled out from under a rock when I apologized for never having played in a symphony orchestra. I shuffled behind the bass drum as if I were crawling back under that same rock.

The piece for the evening was *Fingal's Cave* by Felix Mendelssohn (some guy I'd never heard of). The orchestra musicians were serious middle-aged adults, not casual and smiling as I was used to in jazz bands. I stood about 40 feet from the conductor, all the way in the back feeling isolated and alone. The maestro was the most ominous creature I'd ever seen. His foreign accent blaring over the musicians left me petrified. My only hope was somehow to fake it and go unnoticed.

When the music started, it felt like a train pulling out of a station, leaving me behind. My part looked simple enough—a couple of notes on the bass drum—and I did my best to count the bars of rest. But I'd never done it before. In band you just played right away, as did everyone else, and kept going almost continually, especially in the marches. Now three quarters of the page I was looking at consisted of rests; the remainder was music played by others to let you know where you were.

But those cues didn't help because I couldn't read music.

I just hoped that the grumpy timpanist, only a few feet away, would somehow help me out with a glance, as players did in school band. By waiting for his help I was already too late. The conductor stopped and stared at me over his bifocals. The room waited for one of us to speak. "Bass drum! Where are you?" I was so embarrassed I couldn't say a thing. "Well?"

I cleared my throat: "Well...today's Thursday, which is our spaghetti night at home, and whenever I have spaghetti I feel sleepy afterwards."

The conductor's mouth dropped and he covered a smile with his hand. The whole orchestra laughed; the violinists even tapped their bows on music stands in applause.

Suddenly I was a hero. Even the timpanist smiled. I had turned a dreary rehearsal into a social event. I smiled back at the room. The conductor, whose face relaxed for the first time, glanced at the timpanist and gave me a sympathetic nod.

The next time my cue came the timpanist signaled me with his timpani stick and a nod—and I hit the bass drum in the right place. The conductor smiled, the musicians rustled their feet in appreciation and I relaxed for the first time that night. I had been baptized in the holy waters of classical music. ✻

Zoot Suit, Shades and "The Walk"

I PLAYED ONE OF MY BEST DRUM SOLOS ON A HIGH SCHOOL program when I was 14, imitating Gene Krupa's style with hunched shoulders and a sideways look as if listening to every note I played. An older student walked up to me afterwards. "You play those drums pretty good," he said.

He introduced himself as Don Coy. He wore a tweed sport jacket and silk shirt—a very adult look for a high school student in those days—and spoke authoritatively about jazz. I was pleased to get a compliment from such a sophisticated stranger, until he said, "But I see that you haven't heard the latest bebop drummers."

"What's bebop?" I asked. My focus was still firmly on swing.

"If you like, I'll take you out to hear something."

He invited me to his place, where he introduced me to one-button roll suit jackets, wide-collar shirts and the Windsor-knotted tie. "Cool threads," he called them.

Back home, my father let me borrow a dark brown double-breasted suit. I drowned in the wide shoulders and deep lapels, but the oversize fit resembled the loose zoot suits Don had shown me in a hipster's catalogue. All I had to do was get the jacket shortened.

My father didn't mind—he accepted on faith my jazz mannerisms, like saying "cool" for "yes" and "I'm hip" when I agreed. I already wore outlandishly colored ties and filled the house with the tumult of big band records. Dad's usual response to talk about my world was to nod and scan the floor as if looking for some lost object.

For the wide-collar shirt, rare and expensive in those days, Don showed me how to fold the pointed tip of a collar up and tape it underneath to look wide. My mother ironed the tips while I supervised. I finished off my new image with a pair of shades. My version of a zoot suit was now complete.

But I still needed to learn "The Walk." At Don's house, to the music of Lester Young, he showed me how to walk duck-footed, shoulders slumped, arms immobile at my sides, mouth slack and slightly open. He assured me this would get me in with the black musicians. I practiced at home when no one was around, saying, "Hey man, what's happenin'?"—something else Don had taught me.

On the big night, Don drove me through the heart of Chicago's South Side to the Pershing Hotel at 63rd and Cottage Grove. He told me to put on my shades and walk The Walk. We sauntered through a buzz of nightlife I had seen only in movies—blacks cruising the sidewalk, women in colorful dresses, men in sharp suits with bright ties and two-toned shoes. I felt intoxicated by this new adventure and the knowledge that I was in disguise. No one knew I was really a kid. As we maneuvered into the Pershing Ballroom, I noticed the eyes of a giant bouncer on me. I kept going as if I'd been there many times before.

The room was spacious and darkly lit. People were jitterbugging on the dance floor or standing around in small clusters listening to the music, which was still a hum of background noise. Women's dresses swirled and men's legs and arms flexed like rubber. Long chains hung from their belts and nearly brushed the floor.

A guy in a green suit and horn-rimmed glasses glanced at my suit with approval. "Hey man, what's happenin'," he said, to which I replied, "Everythin's cool," as Don had taught me. I milled through the crowd, careful not to bump anyone, feeling more at home in this congenial atmosphere. At home, magazine cutouts of great jazz musicians filled my bedroom wall, many of them black, some I'd drawn, like trumpeter Roy Eldridge and drummers Big Sid Catlett and Zutty Singleton. They were heroes to me.

I was so overwhelmed that it took me a moment to notice the most virtuosic jazz I'd ever heard: the fast notes of a trumpet dancing over ringing cymbals and a driving bass. I pushed my way to the knee-high bandstand, where I saw that the bassist and drummer were black and the pianist white. None was smiling like players did in swing bands. They appeared deeply concentrated, as if playing for themselves, not us.

This was a new jazz—subtler than swing, playful, varied, full of short, clipped phrases and unexpected rhythmic gestures, virtuosic but never for display. The musicians were talking to each other through their instruments. The drummer's demeanor was also new to me: his movements seemed effortless, almost studious, as he looked down at his cymbal through black wire-rim glasses. He interjected rhythmic comments on his snare drum and tom-toms to encourage whoever was soloing, while keeping an uninterrupted *ding-ding-ga-ding* on the cymbal. In solos he sounded like someone singing, playing figures from his lowest to highest drum and back again, outlining a melody that matched what the sax or trumpet had played.

The alto sax improvisations were especially playful, jumping all over the instrument in unexpected ways, then suddenly turning lyric and smooth with a plaintive sound I had never heard on a horn. The trumpet was not brassy or shrill with high screeching notes, but rather quiet and smoky. The player would embellish a phrase with exciting complexity, sometimes fitting in more notes than seemed possible. The bass player fingered more than four beats to the bar, breaking up the pulse in complex ways, as if he'd just grown three or four extra fingers.

Little did I know I was hearing Charlie Parker on alto, Kenny Dorham on trumpet, Al Haig on piano, Ray Brown on bass and Max Roach on drums. My one visual memory of Parker was a stain on the right jacket pocket of his light brown suit, where a bottle of valve oil was leaking. I was mesmerized and didn't move from the bandstand all night. Don had to drag me back to Brookfield before my parents woke up.

The next day I went to my drums and assumed the calm, studious stance of Max Roach. No more fast exhibitionism common to swing drummers. I played like I was singing the notes, not beating on drums. The model stuck with me through my jazz years. It also showed me I was lyric at heart. This idea stayed with me through the cold days of academic modernism in the 1960s, when computers and mathematical composing methods were in vogue—and my lyricism earned me the enmity of composers who declared melody dead. ❋

Too Green for
Big-Time Jazz

Don and I made other trips to the 63rd and Cottage Grove neighborhood as the year went on. Clubs like the Platinum Lounge, The Bee Hive and Knob Hill were all havens for jazz. One night at the Platinum Lounge, we heard a leading Chicago bebop group, the Joe Daley Trio, with Daley on sax. Don had a brushing acquaintance with Daley, as he seemed to have with most local players, and also knew Daley's drummer, Hal Russell. Don approached Russell during a break and asked if I could "sit in" with the band. This was a common practice; the better jazz musicians all know the standard tunes and tempos and can fit right in without rehearsal. Naturally I was a little nervous as I sat at the drums. This would be my first experience playing with big-time professionals. The musicians waited patiently while I adjusted the setup and lowered the seat. The band played a standard, "I Got Rhythm," in a medium tempo that I negotiated easily. I tried to imitate Max Roach as best I could, even assuming his outward demeanor.

As we finished the tune, Daley gave me an expression known in jazz as The Glare. The Glare is short but clear and carries a deadly message—it's one of those moments in life when you know you're not loved. I wasn't surprised, because I knew I wasn't ready. But my face was hot with embarrassment and I left the bandstand, nodding apologetically to Russell as he came back up on stage. "Nnnn-nn-nice," he said as I passed him, with that special kind of stutter he was well-known for in Chicago jazz circles. But I knew he was just being encouraging. I felt a little embarrassed for Don, too, since he had recommended me.

After we left, Don told me not to feel bad, saying you can only test yourself on the battlefield. He told me about the time drummer Jo Jones threw a cymbal at the feet of a young Charlie Parker, less subtle than The Glare but equally clear, a message to go home and practice. Dizzy Gillespie had also been "cut" once, meaning he was humiliated on the bandstand by a better player in an obscure night-club in Cheraw, South Carolina. Don said the important thing is to dust yourself off and get back to work.

I did exactly that, memorizing all the standard riffs from tunes like Charlie Parker's "Ornithology" and "Donna Lee." And I got comfortable playing "fours," where musicians trade four-bar solos back and forth. I also memorized drum solos by Max Roach and many lesser-known but great drummers, like Joe Harris and Ike Day. I would try to stay in synch with the recording while play-ing—which was tricky, because I had to listen to myself but not drown out the record with my solo. Practicing with recordings built my confidence as I imagined being on the same bandstand with the greats. To this day, I can sing from memory the compli-cated riffs that bebop musicians had devised for each tune—just from having played with Red Rodney and Charlie Parker records in my family's basement.

Within a year I was sitting in at Monday night jam sessions at the Spotlight Lounge on Chicago's North Side. I remember my first night. The players looked back at me and nodded to the rhythm in approval—a far cry from The Glare, which I never suffered again.

My episode with The Glare reminds me of the piano student who went to a great master pianist and played for him. The master asked him what he wanted to do in life. "I want to be a great soloist like you."

"You lack the fire," the master said. "I suggest you do something else."

Years later, after the young man had succeeded as a soloist, he came back to the master. "Remember me? You said I lacked the fire."

The master said, "Oh, I tell that to all my young students." ❧

NOT REALLY THE BLUES

"WHY DO YOU WRITE ABOUT SOMETHING SO MORBID?" MY HIGH school English teacher asked.

She had just read my poem about a fearless individualist climbing a rocky precipice in a storm and pleading to the raging heavens before a giant wave, representing the forces of injustice, swept him away. I was inspired by a dramatic piece of music in a minor key by Stan Kenton's jazz orchestra called "Machito."

My older sister Gloria laughed when I told her about Miss Ewan's response. "When I was in her class she didn't want the girls to wear red or purple because it aroused passion in boys," she said.

But I liked Miss Ewan because she exposed us to literature and encouraged us to write. Our next project was reading great short stories. She said any student who wanted to write a short story would get extra credit. Since my grades needed all the help they could get, I ventured into a story of my own. I had just read a book called *Really the Blues* by jazz clarinet and sax player Mezz Mezzrow. Mezzrow had played in clubs and speakeasies in the Prohibition era, married a black woman and kicked an opium habit.

Inspired by his nonconformist nature and obvious willpower, I wrote a story about a white boxer who marries a black woman and struggles with a cocaine habit. At the climax he loses a big match, but overcomes his addiction with her help, which is his real victory. I called it "Not Really the Blues."

"Michael, I'd like you to see me after class today."

I was sure Miss Ewan was going to tell me I was a gifted writer and wanted me to submit my story somewhere. "Your father is post-master in Brookfield, isn't he?"

"Yes."

"You have a happy home life, don't you?"

"Uh…yeah."

"Then why do you write things like this—prizefighters, interracial marriage, and we don't even think about drugs."

"Well, some people do."

"I'm going to tell you something you won't like. I think you should stop playing the drums. I notice how the other students are nervous and excited when they come out of a lyceum assembly after you've played a solo. I want you to have a talk with Mr. Thompson."

La Rue Thompson was the Dean of Boys, a great teacher and a prince of a human being. When I explained my case, he scanned the floor a moment and said, "Well, Miss Ewan is a little staid in her ways." We agreed that, to keep the peace, I'd keep my fictional inspirations out of her class. ✿

"Who's Rousseau?"

After graduating from high school, I got tired of being myself and spent a year acting like somebody else. I had focused like a professional musician since grade 8, running my band, practicing after school, going into Chicago to hear, meet and finally play with adult jazz musicians.

I'd never really been a normal teenager. School dances, athletics, double dates—I had only seen them from behind my drum set. So I set my drums aside and went to LaGrange Township Junior College for a year. I studied the interesting things I had ignored or skimmed over in high school, like psychology and world literature. I also became an athlete and model student. I became, in other words, normal.

In retrospect, I wanted to be both smarter and dumber than before. I envied students who applied themselves academically and got good grades—the measure of intelligence in school. But I also wanted to lose myself in the persona of a student athlete. I wanted to build up my body and look healthy and gain the admiration of other students (especially girls). For years I'd looked pale from late hours and overwork in Chicago's musical underworld.

So after graduating high school I jogged all summer with an eye toward joining the college track team. My real interest was not in winning, but I liked the special trance of gaining a second wind and feeling I could run forever. In that endorphin-filled state, thoughts about life and drum solos floated by and disappeared like clouds. From what I saw on the track team, my buddies didn't care about secret mental worlds as much as blue and red ribbons.

I usually kept up the rear in our cross-country races, and the coach, Max Armor, would berate me along the way. "Snodgrass"—his pet name for me—"get the damn lead out." Near the finish line I would show off with a big sprint, and he'd say, "I hate to have to tell you that the idea is to use your energy *during* the race, not at the end when you're coming in last and it doesn't matter anymore."

Competitively speaking he was absolutely right. Meditatively speaking he didn't have a clue. I was setting myself up to run for the rest of my life as a way of exercising my spirit. I had read Jean-Jacques Rousseau in philosophy class and liked his idea of a return to nature. I immediately associated that with running in the woods with my shirt off, touching trees and smelling plants. Maybe this communing with intangibles was also a way to keep my creative self alive while giving drumming a rest.

But my spiritual bent was conflicting with a newfound material-ism. You might say I was a budding mystic in Western garb. Half of me was pining for a middle-class existence, the other half trying to insulate myself from it. I wore a white school athletic sweater with sports letters and pins that boasted athletic accomplishments—just like other jocks that girls admired. I had a pretty girlfriend named Julie. She was athletic and quiet, always waiting for me to talk. I spent a year of my life with her, going to dances and talking about who was "really swell" and who was a "loser." And I hung around with track buddies. No more Don, no more zoot suits and dark glasses, no more jazz clubs on Chicago's South Side. But it was fun: late night drive-ins on weekends, popcorn and necking, locker room banter about the Cubs (who couldn't buy a win) and the Bears (who almost went all the way—it was 1950).

But the dreamer in me, who loved the drums and idolized the studious composure of Max Roach, lived only in my head on long cross-country runs. Reality with my fellow runners involved no dreams. When we talked about running one day, I told them I was communing with the elements, and quoted Rousseau about returning to nature. All I got were blank stares. When I told Julie about the conversation, she said, "Who's Rousseau?"

My junior college friends were grooming me for a middle-American existence that sharply contradicted the other American dream, the one I'd loved, of sod-busting independence. But I was enjoying temporary relief from what e.e. cummings calls "the awful responsibility" of being an artist.

As the school year drifted to a close, my friends dispersed and Julie and I drifted apart without the lunchroom and drive-ins to hold us together. Looking back, I find it difficult to remember our conversations. I can picture her in bobby socks, cashmere sweaters and a pretty bow in her hair. I wore penny loafers and school sweaters with the big "L" on them. And I recall the fragrance of her living room, where she kept a quart milk bottle filled with perfumed water behind the couch. But what did we talk about on that couch?

On our last night together, I unleashed my pent-up feelings: "Don't you ever think a thought or have a feeling?" I said. "What goes on in your head all day long?" She just sat on the couch, arms pulling her legs tightly against her chest, head resting sideways on her knees, not moving.

I wish I could go and take back this tirade. Looking back on my year with her, I was a phony, using her as a passport to social acceptance. Now I was taking it out on her, and I'm still ashamed of it. ✻

PART II
1950–1966

"I'M A COMPOSER!"

A FRIEND CONVINCED ME THAT IF I WANTED TO BE A GREAT JAZZ drummer I should expand my knowledge—learn classical percussion playing and other kinds of music. So after I turned 18, I auditioned at the University of Illinois in Champaign-Urbana. I could read only rhythm at the time and couldn't find C on the treble clef, but I guess they thought I had enough talent to catch up.

I was of two minds about studying classical music. The little I'd heard sounded boring, something for gray-haired, dandruffy old people. My attitude got me on scholastic probation almost immediately. In the first six-week grading period I flunked three courses— hygiene, phys ed and band—simply by not attending. I was up late playing gigs at a local club and rolling into school around noon, oblivious that I had already missed class.

"What's happenin' man?" I'd ask as I sauntered up the steps of Smith Music Hall.

"Well, *man*, your theory class happened at 8, and your history class happened at 10. Otherwise you're cool." I wasn't practicing for my marimba or piano lessons and I could barely understand what teachers were saying about harmony and counterpoint. At the end of the semester, my music theory teacher said, "Michael, I'm giving you a D because I think you really tried."

In the second semester, someone told me my percussion teacher Paul Price said, "Oh no, he's back!" In a last-ditch attempt to turn me into a responsible student, he urged me to "come hear your colleagues play in a percussion ensemble concert. You've never been."

So I did. He caught me in the lobby of Smith Music Hall afterwards and asked for my reaction. "You really want to know what I think?" I said. "Well, I was impressed by how well they read the music and could play all the percussion instruments, but frankly I thought the music was terrible."

His expression remained unchanged. He said in a very controlled voice, "Well, why don't you try your hand?" I had never heard that expression before, and looked at him, puzzled.

"If you don't like what you heard, why don't you write what you'd like to hear?"

Celebratory bells went off in my head. I had never even considered writing a piece of music. To me, you had to be dead to compose. Or a genius. As the idea dawned on me, sunlight in the music school hallway seemed to grow brighter, and to this day I can see the radiance of sunbeams streaming through Smith Music Hall's windows.

"How would I start?" I asked.

He took me downstairs to the percussion room and showed me scores by Varèse, Bartok and other moderns. But I was confused. Paul had to explain why so many instruments were listed in the left margin. I was amazed that one person could hear all those parts at once—but then, I'd been knocking myself out for years trying to create ever more complex drum solos with only two arms. With a pencil I could have as many arms as I wanted!

I literally ran to the music store for score paper and started writing my first piece that day. It was for three solo drummers with six accompanying percussionists playing various small instruments. I called it *Three Brothers*. I carried it wherever I went and periodically showed it to Price. He encouraged me to keep going and gave it a run-through with his ensemble when I finished three weeks later. But the solo snare drummer struggled with the extremely fast tempo I had written, and Price suggested it was too fast for all those notes. I walked over to the drummer, took the sticks from his hands and played the part as written. Price frowned at me, but nodded. Afterwards he called me aside and said I should never embarrass a musician in rehearsal. In the jazz world it was customary to get to the point, but I learned that among classical musicians diplomacy came first.

Price premiered *Three Brothers* at the university, with me as one of the soloists. I vividly remember floating out of the music building after that noon performance on the 28th of May, 1951, wearing crepe-soled shoes that made the sidewalk feel like a soft cloud. The lilac bushes were in bloom. I heard myself say, "I'm a composer."

Later that day, Price said he wanted another piece for a fall concert. From that point on I was constantly composing, usually for Price. He recorded and published *Three Brothers* shortly afterwards, and several others have since recorded it. The Percussive Arts Society recently told me it was the most-played percussion ensemble piece in the country.

It's amazing to me that throughout my entire elementary and high school education no one had ever asked me to compose. Music educators themselves don't introduce students to even the most basic composing techniques, and don't expect them to have any talent. What if Paul Price hadn't asked me to write a piece? Would I have stumbled on the idea myself? ✳

JAZZ AND DRUGS 101

IN UNIVERSITY I QUICKLY HOOKED UP WITH THE BEST JAZZ musicians on campus. Several of them were junkies. Cocaine and heroin were essential to what I called "the jazz trance," a belief among players that they had to be high to play. Some used drugs to shut out societal pressures, others to release or pacify demons that blocked creativity. In those days there were plenty of smack-shooting players in jazz to admire. The idea was simply in the air: if you were serious about jazz, you lived the life, and that included drugs.

My attitude was different. I had other ways of altering my mental state. I loved to exercise and ran for miles through the university campus every day. Jogging released endorphins, my own morphine, without interfering with the motor skills I needed to play.

Still, I spent hours after gigs hanging around in clubs and cramped apartments with players who shot up or smoked up. I even held the tourniquet more than once while they looked for the right vein. They didn't mind my being there because I didn't judge them.

Or so I thought. A philosophy student and writer named Barbara Roby was driving us everywhere and stirring up conversations about the meaning of jazz for her first book. She would push her ideas, scanning the horizon with intensely staring eyes.

One night she asked me why I didn't "turn on." I told her I didn't need it. She asked how I knew since I hadn't done it. I said I thought I was strong enough without it, to which she said, "Ah-ha, so you do judge them for what they're doing!"

Our argument turned fierce. She yelled at me, saying it was no sign of strength to resist what I didn't understand—that if I had used drugs and then stopped using them, that would be a sign of strength. "You're an absolutist, Michael, and that's the flaw in your thinking in general."

She was right. My absolutist attitude also told me jazz was richer than classical, simply because musicians created it on the spot. That was just one of my black-and-white ideas about life, all stemming from the notion that a fundamental truth existed. You had to discover that truth and dedicate yourself to it. Did I pick that up from my Catholic upbringing or possibly my father's work ethic?

My philosophy collided with Barbara another time, in a ferocious late-night argument. I argued for survival of the fittest over her communal view of life. I stormed out and talked to myself all the way back to my rooming house several miles away. But gradually I began to question my views on people and politics—that the poor could always pull themselves up by their bootstraps, that America's world-respected government was right, that willpower could change everything. Our midnight debate softened my hard-line views and began my gradual transformation into a classical musician and composer. I realized jazz was not the only "true" music, and that Bach was as alive as Charlie Parker—a life-enhancing discovery.

I also became more human, sensitive to the myriad examples of relativity that I had been blocking out, and saw that multiple viewpoints made life richer and creativity itself possible. As I opened up to my surroundings I learned the value in Mao Zedong's remark, "Let a hundred flowers blossom." ❊

A HEART-STOPPING EVENT

AT THE END OF MY FRESHMAN YEAR, OUR SAX PLAYER, CAL, INVITED us down to West Virginia to celebrate his niece's high school graduation. A couple of players were using, so Cal warned them that the Old-World genteel South was not a good place to get high. Everyone promised to behave.

Cal's family mansion was right out of *Gone with the Wind*. It boasted a wide, winding staircase, glittering chandeliers and paintings of ancestors everywhere. His uncle welcomed us into the front hall with Southern hospitality, introducing us to aunts and cousins and neighbors, who all found it "so nice" that Cal had brought friends home for the big dance. And they were proud of his majoring in business. Seeing him here, I realized how white and Southern he really was, with his drawl and quiet, gentlemanly nature. He was at home.

Cal's niece and her girlfriends, with their ruffled dresses and Pepsodent smiles, seemed interested in us "fine university men." I was chatting with one of them on the night of the dance, sipping a mint julep while my friends were upstairs getting dressed—when a nonchalant voice called me over the banister.

"Oh, Michael, could you come upstairs for a moment?" It was Chris, our horn player. He sounded like he wanted to borrow some toilet article. So I continued talking with our hosts. Then Chris' voice carried an undertone of urgency: "Michael, could you please come upstairs…uh, like immediately?"

I excused myself and went upstairs, where Chris, ashen-faced, led me into the master bedroom. Stretched out on the floor was Cal, blue and barely breathing, a syringe lying beside him. "Oh my God," I said, "Let's get him in a cold shower."

"No!" said Chris. "That'll kill him. We have to walk him. Quick, take his other arm." We lifted Cal off the floor and walked him back and forth. Chris kept pleading, "C'mon, Cal, don't die . . . we're here Cal . . . stay with us."

Someone called from downstairs. "Time to go to the dance, boys. Can't keep the girls waiting." They giggled.

"In a minute," we said.

After a few trips across the carpet Cal began to murmur and cough, some color coming back into his face. We sat him down on the bed. He looked around until a beautific smile came over his face. "Man," he mumbled, " 'at's some wunnerful shit."

If I weren't so relieved I would have brained him.

Chris and I got him cleaned up and dressed. Miraculously he looked quite good. We were wet with perspiration and had to change our shirts.

At the dance we kept an eye on Cal. His Southern social skills came through admirably, though anyone who knew to look could see that glassiness in his eyes and catch a slur in his voice. When we finally saw him dancing across the floor, Chris and I took a full breath for the first time all evening.

I didn't see Cal after he graduated in 1953. When I got the Pulitzer Prize in 1978 he called and asked me to look him up on my next visit to New York City. We eventually met at a coffeehouse and recalled old times. He looked impressive in his grey business suit, white shirt and striped tie—the model of Wall Street efficiency. He was assistant director of marketing at Chase Manhattan Bank. ❧

TAPS FOR BIG SID

I HEARD THE GREAT JAZZ DRUMMER BIG SID CATLETT PLAY AT THE
Civic Opera House in Chicago in 1951. I was disappointed that Big
Sid didn't come out for the second half, so I slipped backstage to
find out why. Assuming my usual "I belong here" attitude, I mingled
with the musicians and overheard them speaking in subdued tones.
Someone asked where Big Sid was and a man answered by tilting his
head toward a circular metal staircase.

I knew something was wrong, but couldn't place it. When no one
was looking, I sneaked up the staircase to the opera house stage where
Big Sid was stretched out on a nine-foot grand piano in the wings.

Back-lit by the stage nightlight was a man playing taps slowly
and softly over Big Sid's body. I hid in a fold of curtains, watching
from about 15 feet away. A cloth cap hung on the end of the trumpet
to mute the sound. The player was a black shadow in the semi-dark-
ness and sounded like Miles Davis or Kenny Dorham.

I didn't move until he finished his tribute, which must have lasted
two or three minutes. Then I slipped back down the winding stairs
and out the stage door. ❧

VERBAL SPARRING
WITH JOHN CAGE

I HIT IT OFF WITH JOHN CAGE THE FIRST TIME WE MET. I WAS playing his music at the University of Illinois in 1952. Cage and I struck up a conversation because he liked my piece *Three Brothers*, which he said was obviously inspired by brotherhood. I didn't tell him that my real inspiration had been Woody Herman's *Four Brothers*.

Between rehearsals, I tried to spark a healthy debate with Cage about composing. I respected his experimental nature but disputed his apparent disregard for the past. (He was already world-famous for his work, *4'33"*, a piece of absolute silence.) I wondered if he was ignorant of Western music's vast history, as I'd been only a year before—so I stood up for the old masters over coffee at Prehn's, a campus café.

Cage's face remained calm, even stoic, and he spoke gently and quietly, ignoring the noisy talk and bursts of laughter around us. My attempts at logical argument seemed wasted. Linear thought was just not part of his discourse.

At one point he asked me for a piece of blank music paper. I produced one and watched him shake pepper on it. He carefully turned the page around and slid it across the table. I looked at the black and gray flakes. "You mean that the flakes on the lines and spaces are naturals and those in between are sharps and flats?" I asked.

"That's up to you," he said.

Cage's way of reasoning reminded me of aikido. Instead of attacking or defending, aikido masters use their opponent's aggression to throw them off balance and gain the upper hand. "Teaching your opponent the error of his ways," an aikido expert once called it. This defined Cage, who simply refused to fight. When I thrust an idea at him he would sidestep it and redirect my words into a point he wanted to make.

Walking back to the music school, I was still thrusting and missing when Cage stopped to point out a light layer of snow on the grass. "Notice how some of the blades of grass show through the snow and others do not," he said.

We continued on our way in silence. ❉

"It's Not Personal"

I WAS NERVOUS THE FIRST TIME I REHEARSED WITH THE UNIVERSITY of Illinois student orchestra. Paul Price stood at my side coaching me. He was on a mission to show the music world that percussionists were serious musicians who deserved the same respect as string and woodwind and brass players. He always pushed us to make the best impression possible.

I had only a simple triangle part, but when my entrance came I played too softly. The conductor, Bernard Goodman, stopped the orchestra and said, "Triangle, you didn't play."

"I *did* play," I said loudly.

Paul elbowed me and said, "Thank you, maestro."

Afterward he took me aside. "You never talk back to the conductor. He's short on time and is only interested in results. When he singles you out he isn't criticizing you. Remember, *it's not personal.*"

I was still an informal and outspoken jazz musician. But I admired Jack McKenzie, the orchestra's principal percussion player and timpanist, so I took him as a model on answering conductors with control and respect, never making excuses. Soon I was taking barbs like, "Learn to play your instrument," "Pay attention" and "Wake up!" on the chin like a professional, no matter how unfair they seemed.

A few months later Jack and I were accepted into the Festival Orchestra at Tanglewood. Now we were playing with the country's best young musicians under world-class conductors. One of our first pieces was Aaron Copland's *Billy the Kid*. Conducting the piece himself, Copland ran into problems with the printed parts. Markings and cuts scribbled in by ballet orchestras threw off our timing, leading us to play in the wrong places. It was a mess. Copland kept stopping to sort out discrepancies between the score and the parts, and finally gave up, telling senior conductors Jean Morel and Leonard Bernstein, "I can't do this."

Bernstein had already conducted and recorded *Billy the Kid*, and quickly took over. But he hit the same obstacle, stopping to correct people and clarify entrances. His irritation only grew. When we came to the big gunfight scene, featuring percussion in tricky syncopated cowboy shootout rhythms, I was on snare drum and Jack on bass drum. Bernstein cued us by drawing and aiming imaginary pistols, but Jack came in at the wrong place. Bernstein yelled, "No!"

We started again. He cued us and again Jack was off. Bernstein slapped the score shut so hard that the conductor's stand flew. The concertmaster jerked his violin away just in time.

"This piece is off the program," Bernstein declared and stormed offstage, firing murderous glances at Jack.

Jack got the message—it was his fault. Fuming, he lunged at the maestro. I'd never seen him like this. I caught him by the arm as he said, "It *wasn't* my fault."

"Jack, *Jack,*" I said. "*It's not personal!*"

I doubt that Bernstein, who later apologized to the orchestra and put the piece back on the program, ever knew how close he'd come to a broken nose. ✳

BRAHMS MADE ME JUMP AND RUN

THE FIRST TIME I HEARD THE BOSTON SYMPHONY PLAY LIVE, I WAS so excited that I jumped up and ran. It was Brahms' *Symphony No. 2* in the open-air shed at Tanglewood, under Charles Munch. I sat in the front row, about 15 feet away with the full weight of the music right in my lap. The Romantic beauty of the piece and the fullness of the sound transfixed me, but the ending was the most powerful. The symphony peaked in a giant buildup of horns and trombones that rose in harmonic tension and ended in an intense flourish. All the musicians seemed to sing as one. The audience rose to its feet before hearing the last notes, applauding and shouting with the final crash.

I jumped up and ran out of the shed, across the lawn and down to the road. I bolted through the gate, passing Nathaniel Hawthorne's red house and sprinting the quarter mile down the dirt road to the Stockbridge Bowl lake. Standing on the end of the pier I yelled as loud as I could: *"I'm going to be a composer!"*

My voice bounced back at me from the surrounding mountains. Or was that just my imagination? ✻

MY LESSONS WITH
MILHAUD

LIKE A LOT OF MUSICIANS IN THE '50S, I ADMIRED THE FRENCH composer Darius Milhaud. I was thrilled when I got a scholarship to study composition with him at the Aspen Festival in the summer of 1953.

I soon learned that the best part of working with him was impressing others by talking about it. The fact is, he taught me nothing. Our lessons were group sessions where, one by one, we showed Milhaud our work for the week and listened to his comments. That format is fine if the teacher is sensitive to the feelings and level of development of each student. But that wasn't Milhaud.

I learned more from Hal Overton, the best student in the class, who also played jazz piano. He would play his work in progress on the keyboard and Milhaud would say, "Good," but add nothing to help Hal improve it. One day I got my chance to show Milhaud a half-finished piece for percussion ensemble. I explained what I was doing and intended to do next. He glanced at it quickly. "Edgard Varèse, Lou Harrison, John Cage, Henry Cowell, all these and more have written many pieces for percussion, and I have written my *Christopher Colombo*," he said. "After all that, what do you expect to add to percussion that has not already been done?"

I was crushed of course, but didn't let it show.

I did learn something from our exchange—that the only way to teach composition is to make specific and useful criticisms based on a student's strong points, however thinly developed they may be. This is how the great composition teacher Eugene Weigel nurtured my work at the University of Illinois. Sympathetic to my vision—however naïve it was—he came up with creative ways to make it richer. He could actually teach people how to conceive and develop a musical idea. When I mention Wiegel's name, most people say, "Who?" But when I mention Milhaud they look as if I just stepped out of *Gramophone* magazine. Fame doesn't make someone a good teacher—and their names are only useful if you like dropping them. ✻

Big-Rig Genius

Heading home from the Berkshire Music Festival in 1952, I hitched a ride with a truck driver who was carting a dozen new cars to California. He wore a T-shirt and jeans on his thin frame and had several days' growth of beard. Nothing about him seemed special. But whenever we stopped at a red light, his head dropped and his eyes closed. Even at stop signs, if there happened to be a lineup, his head would drop for a few seconds. He always awoke as the traffic began to move and was obviously an excellent driver.

After a while I asked him what he was doing. At first he didn't understand because his habit was so reflexive.

"Oh," he said finally, "I'm sleeping." When I expressed my disbelief, he said, "If I can get these cars to California a day early I get a big bonus, so I drive straight through."

"But don't you ever stop for a night's sleep?"

"About once a day I pull over to the shoulder and sleep for an hour or two, then drive on. The little sleeps I get at lights and traffic backups are enough for me." I asked how he knew to wake up in time, as if someone poked him when the light changed. "I don't know. All I know is, I'm gonna get these cars to the West Coast in three days any way I can."

I'd worked with great conductors that summer like Charles Munch, Leonard Bernstein, Jean Morel, Thor Johnson and Loren Maazel, who executed dozens of tempo changes with infallible timing from memory. This truck driver impressed me no less with his muscle response and unique inner timer. Conducting a symphony orchestra is a huge task, but no less daunting is driving a big-rig safely across the country without a night's sleep. ✳

ADVICE FROM A STRANGER

I WAS EATING SOUP IN THE TANGLEWOOD CAFETERIA ONE SUMMER day in 1954, when a stranger sat down and struck up a conversation. Decked out in suit and tie, he was obviously a visitor to the Berkshire Music Festival. He asked about my studies and I said I had just finished university. My next stop was the draft and two years with the Seventh Army Symphony in Stuttgart, Germany. Friends in the orchestra were putting through a request to get me in after 16 weeks of basic training.

"Let me give you a piece of advice," the man said. "When you enter the Army they will give you a battery of tests. One of them is the Morse code test. Fuck it up! Good radio men are hard to find and musicians always do well on that test. If they assign you to radio school it will be hard to get you out."

The day after I was drafted, I went through three days of Army placement testing. I went a step further than the stranger's advice and did well only on music-related tests. On the Morse code test— all easy questions on simple rhythms—I made a point of screwing up. But I made sure to get the occasional answer right to avoid arousing suspicions.

After basic training I was sent directly to the Army symphony, where I spent 13 months touring Germany, Great Britain,

Scandinavia and other European countries as a kind of US Army goodwill ambassador. A few weeks after I started, the conductor told me about a clarinetist he'd been trying to get transferred from Mannheim. The problem: the clarinetist was a radio operator, a priority Army assignment that is rarely overridden. It was six months before we finally got him.

I later learned that my Tanglewood cafeteria advisor was none other than Howard Taubman, the senior music critic for the *New York Times*. So I can't say that I never learned anything from a critic. ❈

AT WAR WITH THE ARMY

MUSICIANS ARE BY NATURE NONVIOLENT. BUT THAT DOESN'T MEAN they won't fight. Given a natural enemy—like the military—musicians can be awesome adversaries.

The US Army had set up an orchestra in Stuttgart to travel around Europe and show that Americans could be cultured. As one German official put it, "We knew you could make automobiles, but *this...!*"

Audiences liked the Seventh Army Symphony, but the officers kept a suspicious eye on us in case we slacked off or weren't "real soldiers." The Army already resented our extra per diem pay, free time, lack of inspections and military maneuvers—not to mention nights in hotels and private homes. And we, in spite of our fortunate circumstances, resented the Army in return.

Instead of receiving thanks for a job well done, we faced threats of the symphony being disbanded and musicians forced to pick up rifles and do maneuvers in the field. So we led a schizoid existence and looked for ways to preserve our sanity.

One day a violinist showed up at rehearsal pulling a stuffed bear on red wheels. The bear stood about two feet high and looked at us with soulful eyes through rich brown fur. It quickly became the orchestra's mascot. We named him Forward and took him on tour wherever we went. We even rolled him into the mess hall to irritate regular soldiers. They thought we were weird anyway, so why not give them something to talk about.

As word of our bear got around, some symphony players criticized our "childish behavior" and suggested we get rid of Forward. Instead, we decided Forward needed company, and bought another considerably larger bear named Onward. Now there were two.

Meanwhile, an outstanding violist named George Andrix from military intelligence in Frankfurt had been visiting us to play string quartets. We tried to get him in the symphony, but Frankfurt refused. George liked our bears so much, he bought one for himself. His was mid-sized, named Sideways, and it joined him everywhere he went—into town, the cafeteria, movies, even his office at intelligence headquarters.

One day his commanding officer in Frankfurt called him in.

"Andrix, you've been bringing a toy bear to work in the morning," he said.

"Yes, sir."

"You bought this bear for a refugee child?"

"No, sir."

"Then why do you have it?"

"I like bears."

The next morning George was sent to the base psychiatrist, who read the commander's report. "Did you buy this bear because you were lonely?"

"No sir, I just like bears. Wanna meet him?"

"You mean you brought him here?" The doctor watched George wheel Sideways into the office. Soon the doctor was also enchanted with the bear. "Well, you're certainly eccentric but I can't say you're crazy."

George was soon shipped to the Seventh Army Symphony, which his commanding officer called "the one place that seems to want you." He showed up in Stuttgart with customary backpack, rifle, viola and bear. The military police didn't want to let him on the base, so we came down to clear him through the gate.

George's victory over military intelligence boosted our spirits and unleashed a flood of new bears. There came Backwards, Outward, Upward and the first female, a blonde, named Inward. Someone even found a tiny bear the size of a hand and called him Help.

By now Seventh Army headquarters was seething. Rumor had it they were sending a tough officer to "shape up the Symphony."

His name was Major Lokker (we called him Foot Locker), a gung-ho veteran of several military campaigns. Word was he would force inspections—spotless barracks, short haircuts, standing at attention—things we hadn't seen since basic training. So we decided to do it right. Bears were members of the symphony, and they too would stand inspection. We dressed them in military hats and ties and stacked them on top of each other in the middle of the barracks floor, where they couldn't be missed. They almost reached the 14-foot ceiling.

Come zero hour, we were shining at attention as Major Lokker stormed down the hall toward our beachhead. He made a sweeping circle around the room—avoiding even a glance at the bears—and walked out as if he were on wheels himself. Was this veteran warrior, who had led a company at the invasion of Normandy, so intimidated by the bears he couldn't even look at us?

But one day we went too far. On a trip to play at London's Royal Festival Hall, we put Onward and Forward onstage peeking out of the wings at the audience. Photos on the front page of the *Guardian* showed us pulling bears across the airfield under the headline, "Bears Stand Guard While Soldiers Play." That snapped it. Humiliated, the Army sent down a directive when we returned to Stuttgart: "Commencing immediately, no manikins larger than pocket-size will accompany the symphony on tour."

Don't ask me why they stopped at pocket-size, but that was their mistake. We all went out and bought puppets, launching a new campaign in our war with the Army.

Officers couldn't grasp how we dared to defy orders that others obeyed and feared. But to a musician, the only authorities are Beethoven, Brahms, Bartok, and other musical greats—leaders far more demanding than anyone in Army uniform. ❋

Journey to
San Marco

When the Army gave me a week's leave in the spring of 1955, my Chicago relatives told me to visit our family in Italy posthaste. I was not pleased of course. A young man of 23 doesn't want to use his first free time in Europe to visit relatives!

But I knew I'd never live it down if I didn't go. My father came to the United States with his mother and four siblings in 1907 when he was five years old. I was the first of our family to return to Europe, so I was naturally appointed to visit the Colagrossi clan in their home-town of San Marco in the province of Foggia, the ankle of Italy.

Making the long trip south, I rode the trains from Stuttgart to Rome, Rome to Naples, Naples to Foggia. From there, a local driver took me up and down the rugged mountain roads of this rich grape-growing region to San Marco, perched on a mountaintop.

When the car dropped me off, I walked into the heart of the lit-tle village. I asked in my broken, minimal Italian for my great aunt Michelina Conte. Impressed by my windbreaker and sneakers, vil-lagers surrounded me, jabbering in an impossible-to-understand dia-lect, trying to figure out who I was. Finally a man said, "Ahhh…" He smiled, embraced me and took me to a house where a large family was ecstatic to see a relative from Chicago.

We commenced three days of nonstop eating and drinking. I remember a parade of rich lasagnas; cannelloni; pastas with green and red sauce; fresh veal and chicken cooked in homemade marsala; goat's cheese and provolone on freshly baked crusty bread; and olives in spicy oil, accompanied by a continual river of yellow and amber wines from local grapes. Naturally we all took dozens of photographs of each other as we walked around, trading stories and visiting the family cemetery.

Finally, they saw me off on a local bus to Foggia, which met the train to Naples and on to Stuttgart. I developed the photographs and mailed them to Chicago. Family obligation fulfilled!

My father promptly wired back: "You went to the wrong San Marco."

They had forgotten to tell me there are two San Marcos in the province of Foggia: San Marco in Lamis and San Marco la Catola. The people in Lamis had considered me an offshoot of their many relatives in Chicago, a good enough reason to celebrate.

My relatives in Chicago cried, "You have to go back!" The next year, I made the demanding trip again—this time to San Marco la Catola. The whole town was waiting to greet me, the important Colagrossi dignitary. Some of their smiling, sun-tanned faces reminded me of my sister Gloria, with the same eyes but a larger bone structure.

Out of the crowd swaggered a short man with a hooked nose and sharp chin, pipe gripped tightly in his teeth. He wore a dusty and tattered American-style overcoat. "What seems to be the problem here?" he asked in accented English. He shot out his hand like a businessman. "Frank S. Oliver's the name."

What luck! A born-and-raised San Marco man who had lived in New York for years. Frank was now the village hero. Anyone who wanted to talk to me or invite me over went through him, and he milked it to the hilt. His favorite response: "Before I answer that question, we need more wine and cake."

One of the delights of my visit was listening to Frank tell stories that recklessly blended myth and reality. He claimed that he'd played oboe in Toscanini's first orchestra in New York, and that the maestro kept him on because he liked the way Frank, a trained barber, shaved him. On the balcony of my little room, Frank recounted his near-discovery of a hidden treasure.

Pointing down the mountain, he said, "Ya' see that Roman arch down there? Well, one night I had a dream there was gold buried under that arch. I woke my brother, got a pick, a shovel and a lantern and went down there, and we dug and we dug, and all of a sudden, bang! We hit somethin' hard. A chest! We dug around it and pulled it out.

"It had a lock on it, but it was broken!" His eyes squinted: "Some other som-na-bitch had the same dream, got there before us and got all the gold!"

I laughed until tears streamed down my face.

Before leaving Italy, I confirmed one important thing: the secret to my grandmother's unique tomato sauce. The villagers would quick-fry a few pork chops and let them stew in the sauce all day to enrich the flavor. So I make what I consider to be the best pasta sauce around, although my wife says it tastes like tar. ✻

An American Saint
in Paris

VISITING PARIS FOR THE FIRST TIME, I WAS EAGER TO MEET ONE OF
the famously sexy French women I had heard so much about. I knew
no one, but figured I might catch someone's eye in an outdoor café.
I found a cozy one near the opera house and ordered a glass of Pernod, knowing it was a favorite afternoon drink in France. I thought
that made me a very cool 23-year-old. As I scanned the crowd, an
attractive brunette in a smart suit sat down near me.

To my surprise I didn't have to do a thing. She ordered a cup
of espresso, looked my way and smiled. Could I be this lucky? I
smiled back and she invited me over with a tilt of her head. I didn't
think she was a prostitute, but I wondered what made me so irre-
sistible. She easily opened up, speaking in English about her job
and her problems.

She said she was struggling with her life and her relationships. She
also doubted whether she still believed in God—could I help her?
Naturally, I was full of religious advice. I told her how important it
was to believe in herself first, which would help her believe in others.
And I was sure God was with her even when she wasn't sure about
Him. A glow came over her face and I knew I was scoring big points.

A young man walked up and kissed her on both cheeks in the French style. She introduced him as her boyfriend, saying how kind and helpful I had been. He thanked me with a smile and a handshake. She called the waiter over, got the bill and insisted on paying for my drink.

"I want to thank you, Father," she said. "I will always remember our talk." And the couple walked off.

Father? Puzzled, I finished my drink and went to the café bathroom. In the mirror, I saw my high-collared black raincoat covering all but two inches of my white shirt. She thought I was a priest!

I never did meet a woman in Paris, but I went back to Stuttgart with a story that left my Army buddies in stitches. ❋

GREENBERG'S LAW

LLOYD GREENBERG ALWAYS SEEMED TO HAVE MORE MONEY THAN the rest of us in the Seventh Army Symphony. He'd show up with a new single-lens reflex camera, or a new clarinet, or an Italian motor scooter. I began to wonder if he was moonlighting for the CIA. So I asked him how he could afford such luxuries on our meager pay.

"I buy only what I need and I never buy cheap," he said. "Good things last for years and I can usually resell when I'm finished with them."

His philosophy was different from what my mother had taught me. She would buy me the cheapest pair of shoes and say they were as good as the expensive ones with a fancy name. When I complained about my cramped feet she would say, "You've got to break them in." I would limp around for weeks until the shoes were forced out of shape and began to feel right. A few months later they would split open and she would have to buy me a new cheap pair.

Moving to New York in 1956 I decided to apply "Greenberg's Law" by spending more and getting the best. I had come into $95 insurance money on a lost parcel of clothing sent from home. My winter coat was gone, so I went to the big department stores to check out styles and prices. (A high quality men's wool coat in those days ran around $50.) Next I tried the walk-ups in the discount-priced garment district on Seventh Avenue, where clothes were a steal.

I even visited exclusive shops on Fifth Avenue. One fancy store displayed a beautiful coat in the window made of vicuna, a new word to me. I strolled in wearing my scruffy corduroy jacket and baggy pants and asked to see it. The salesman looked me over: "Do you really think you're ready for vicuna?" Undaunted, I looked at the price tag—$400! I tried it on and saw him smirking at me in the mirror. How could I get out of this? I noticed a slight droop in the padded shoulders and realized that the soft material probably wasn't durable. (From my coat research, I knew that any soft material, like cashmere, was better if blended with sturdy wool.)

So I took it off, handed it back in a perfunctory manner and said, "Nice coat, but it'll never hold its shape," and walked out.

By now I was an authority on overcoats, and friends were consulting me for advice. I had just discovered a Brooks Brothers outlet on lower Fifth Avenue selling quality clothes at a discount. I took my roommate, clarinetist Arthur Bloom, and he bought a cashmere and wool coat for $92.50. John Palanchian, a violinist friend, liked Art's coat and bought one too. I brought in more friends. I was virtually working as a sales broker for Brooks Brothers. Yet I still hadn't seen the right coat for me.

One day I got a call from Jerry, the head salesman at Brooks, telling me to come down. He showed me a dark charcoal cashmere and lambswool-blend coat with hand-stitching, slightly tapered in an elegant design. I hesitated to ask the price. I looked at Jerry forlornly: "How much?"

"Don't ask," he said. "For you, $92.50."

I wore that coat for 10 years and it never lost its shape. When the cuffs finally started to fray and the length went out of style, my wife turned up the cuffs, shortened the length and I wore it for another five years. Finally, after a decade and a half, I gave it away to a needy composition student.

Someone once asked my wife, "Is Michael a careful shopper?"

"When he wants a new coat he starts by going to examine the sheep in the field!" ✿

MY FIRST NEW YORK
REVIEW

AFTER A FEW MONTHS IN NEW YORK, I WAS LAMENTING MY INABILITY
to break in as a composer. My roommate Art Bloom suggested giving a score to conductor David Broekman, who ran "Music in the
Making," a modern music series at the Cooper Union School of Art.

I phoned Broekman and dropped off my *Chamber Music for Four
Drums and String Quintet.* The next day he phoned and asked me to
send the performance parts as soon as possible: 12 first violins, 10
second violins and so on, enough for a full string orchestra.

"Wait a minute," I said. "This piece is for string quintet, not string
orchestra."

"I know that, but I want to do it with the whole orchestra." I asked
when the first rehearsal would be. "The same day as the concert," he
said. I was astonished.

"These must be pretty good musicians," I said.

"Of course, they're professionals."

In fact they were the same musicians who played under Toscanini
in the NBC Orchestra. When I walked into the Cooper Union concert hall on the morning of the concert, Broekman was taking them
through a sight-read. They sounded wonderful.

Broekman called me on onstage to play my solo part. I felt immensely comfortable playing with musicians who seemed to understand exactly what I wanted. After going through the piece a couple of times, Broekman said, "That's it. See you tonight."

I loved the intensity of it—playing for a New York audience with virtually no rehearsal and taking for granted that it would be good. In fact, it was a terrific performance and I felt tremendously inspired. I took several bows as the players shuffled their feet in appreciation.

I could hardly sleep that night, riding high on the music. The next day, Art came bounding up the stairs of our third-floor walk-up on West 75th Street and made an announcement: "You got three paragraphs in the *Herald Tribune*."

Surprised, I said, "Why do you count the paragraphs?"

He glanced at me with an oh-my-you-are-naïve look and said, "In New York, you count the paragraphs."

I recalled my first review ever, after a jazz concert at the University of Illinois union building. A fellow musician told me our band received a good mention in the *Daily Illini*. I looked at him, puzzled, wondering why anyone would care what a newspaper said about a performance.

In time I came to appreciate reviewers who mix opinion with detailed descriptions of music. But as I found out, readers don't always care. One night at a party a friend congratulated me on "the great review you got in *The New Yorker*." I was puzzled because the review had dismissed my piece, *Déjà vu*, for "serving herbs for dinner instead of meat and potatoes." But it had taken the critic more than half a column of text to say so. I guess my friend Art was right—in the end, people do count the paragraphs. ❈

PREMIERE AT THE FIVE SPOT CAFÉ

VIOLIST MANNY VARDI LIKED MY TUNED DRUM PLAYING SO MUCH that he invited me to his house in New Jersey to demonstrate what the viola could do.

"I think a piece for those tuned drums and viola would make a very good combination," he said after hearing me play these drums with the NBC Orchestra in January of 1957. That was six months after I arrived in New York.

I was overwhelmed by his virtuosity and warmth of tone as he played the Bach *Chaconne* and some Paganini caprices, challenging music for the violin and almost unheard of on the viola.

I fell in love with the viola that day and grew excited at the prospect of writing for Manny, who had a multi-record deal with MGM Records. He even gave me the recording date as if the piece were finished. I said, "You better wait till you see it to know if you like it."

He said something I'll never forget: "I'll like it!"

The remark stunned me. This has to be a really good piece, I thought, because that's what he expects.

We recorded my *Variations for Four Drums and Viola* for MGM Records in the fall of 1957 and gave the first live performance at New

York's Five Spot Café. As it happened, John Coltrane and Thelonius Monk were playing nights at the Five Spot that week, and I was lucky enough to hear them. After that, Manny arranged many New York–area concerts for us. *Variations* lay fallow for years after that because it was too challenging for most violists at the time. (The publisher said to me, "Nice piece, Michael, but who'll be able to play it besides you and Vardi?") One exception was violist Bernie Zaslov, with whom I played several concerts. Eventually others picked up the work until it entered the repertoire of violists around the world. Today it's a staple on viola recitals and my most-performed chamber piece.

Manny gets much of the credit, not just for giving *Variations* a terrific start, but for believing in it before the first note was written. ✳

THE STRIPPER AND
WEST SIDE STORY

THIS STORY IS FOR ANYONE WHO HAS EVER SAID, "OH, IT'S JUST A LITTLE JOB. NOTHING IMPORTANT."

Like every other newcomer in New York I had to start at the bottom. During my first barren months in the city, I got a job playing a wedding in Long Island, where my drums were stolen out of the bandleader's car. Without an instrument or a reputation, I was struggling to make ends meet.

Then the contractor for the *West Side Story* orchestra on Broadway called me. The jazz drummer in Leonard Bernstein's new musical wanted to take his two-week vacation and couldn't find a substitute. The problem was that Broadway show subs get no rehearsal and have to sight-read cold the first night. No one wanted to take the chance. They called me because they were out of options and ready to try a new face in town. They got my name from Juilliard, where I had just auditioned for a master's degree. (I didn't accept their scholarship because I decided to freelance.)

So I went down to the Wintergarden Theater that night and met the drummer, Nat Foodman, who invited me to sit behind him and watch him play the show. The music mixed big band jazz with modern classical style, complex rhythms and meters, fast stick changes, extra percussion instruments and cues to the stage for set changes. "What do you think?" he said afterwards. "Can you do it?"

"Yes, I think so, but I have questions." I kept him in the theater till after midnight.

"Well," he said, "as far as I'm concerned you've got the job."

"But you haven't heard me play."

"I don't have to. You asked all the right questions. But you still have to be approved by Max."

This was Max Goberman, reputed at the time to be the only conductor to have recorded all of Haydn's symphonies. Bernstein wanted a classical conductor in the pit for *West Side Story*.

I met Goberman the next night at intermission. He was a stern man with a goatee and a hard glare, typical of Old-World conductors who bite people's heads off at the slightest provocation. Arms crossed, he said, "Nat seems to like you. But I have one question: This is not a typical musical. Have you ever played anything at all like it?"

Allow me to flash back to the summer of 1952, when I was 20 years old and playing in Tanglewood's Berkshire Festival Orchestra. The percussion section rehearsed every morning at nine under BSO timpanist Roman Schultz. One morning Schultz asked if any of us played jazz. I raised my hand. "There's a club called The Showboat across the state line in New York," he said. "Their drummer is sick and they need a sub. They'll send a car. Think you can do it?"

"Sure," I said.

The drive from Lenox was about two hours. At The Showboat, the manager showed me the curved bar where I would play with a jazz trio. He told me my main job was to play for a stripper. I followed him to a change room and saw an attractive, rather flashy woman of about 35 sitting at a mirror. She seemed comfortable being half naked as she put on a long, flaming red wig and makeup to disguise a bruise.

"Jilly, say hi to Mike. He's your drummer tonight."

I gleaned from his deferential manner that she wielded influence at the club, and was possibly part owner. She asked with authority if I had ever played for a stripper.

"No," I said.

She sized me up and down. "Okay, don't worry about it. Just keep your eyes on me and catch all my bumps and grinds."

I assured her my eyes would be glued to her every move.

I played one set out front with the jazz trio before showtime in the back. I was almost as nervous about playing for Jilly as I had been the week before playing Hindemith's *Mathis der Mahler* with the Festival Orchestra under Lorin Maazel. At curtain time I was as alert as I had ever been for a performance.

The seven-piece show band started a raunchy and boisterous little tune as Jilly moved onstage with a flourish. I emphasized her every move with as much drama as possible. Boom! Bang! Ga-boom! Da-da-da-DUT! Crash! My cymbals rang and the stage vibrated with the impact of the drums. She couldn't move an eyebrow without hearing a rim shot or a bass drum thud.

"Honey," she said afterward, "you're the best I've ever had." (Yes, her actual words!) "How would you like the job in the club?"

I was flattered and almost tempted. "I have a scholarship at Tanglewood and that's a full-time job for me right now."

"Well, just remember you've got the job whenever you want it."

They drove me back early the next morning, just in time for the percussion sectional. The first words out of Schultz's mouth: "I hear things went well at The Showboat last night."

"Yeah," I said, surprised. Why would the Boston Symphony timpanist care about a gig in a nightclub?

After rehearsal, Boston Symphony Managing Director Thomas D. Perry stopped me on my way to the cafeteria.

"Hello, Michael," he said. (How did he know my name?) "I hear you did a good job at The Showboat."

Now I'm really curious. "Yes, I think it went well."

"Listen, in a few weeks we're doing the first professional premiere of Bernstein's new opera, *Trouble in Tahiti*, and it calls for a percussionist who can play both classical and jazz. Would you like to do it?"

"Sure," I said.

Later that month, we performed the opera, a challenge I enjoyed.

Flash forward to 1958, where steely-eyed Max Goberman is asking if I've ever played anything like *West Side Story*. I searched my memory. "Well, I was the percussionist in the premiere of Bernstein's *Trouble in Tahiti* at Tanglewood in 1952."

"You were?" he asked. "Well, all right." He shook my hand and gave me a rare smile.

I not only played Foodman's two weeks of *West Side Story* but finished the show's run for the remaining nine months on Broadway.

A little voice inside me said, "Thank you, Jilly." ✳

SMOKING UP TO PLAY VIOLA

PEOPLE OFTEN ASK WHAT INSPIRES ME AS A COMPOSER, AND I HAVE to say it's the performer for whom I'm writing. A soloist like flutist Marina Piccinini or violist Rivka Golani can spark my creative best. Marina sent my imagination in new directions by playing the early drafts of *Wild Riot of the Shaman's Dreams* as I wrote it. Rivka filled my studio with her paintings to influence the mood of *Chaconne*. Both keep the works alive by playing them and revive them when they lie fallow.

But not all encounters with musicians have such happy endings. One evening in New York, a soloist who was about to play my *Variations for Four Drums and Viola* rolled a joint, lit it and smoked up in front of me.

"But you have a concert to play in an hour," I said.

"The way I look at it," he said, "if I feel good, the audience will feel good."

At the concert he felt very good indeed, making my 17-minute piece last 21 minutes. I squirmed as people around me rustled uncomfortably. I was even tempted to stop the performance and started having second thoughts about this piece.

After the concert I decided to pull it out of circulation. Then serendipity struck. *Variations* was played the very next night by the Chamber Music Society of Lincoln Center at Tully Hall. These players, percussionist Richard Fitz and violist Walter Trampler, were among the world's best. They were sober and the performance was stunning.

How could the same piece sound like it was written by two different composers? Obviously the performer is co-creator of the music. The best go beyond the written notes and hear things the composer never imagined, even change the music's very nature—like an alchemist transforming base metals into gold. ✳

CASTING A SPELL ON BACH

WHEN THE UNIVERSITY OF LOUISVILLE ASKED ME TO GIVE A TALK
on Tradition and Memory, I asked for a pianist who felt at home in
different styles—baroque, classical, Romantic and modern. They
gave me a graduate student named Jeff Myers.

At the talk, I asked Jeff to sit in a chair facing the audience and
play a Bach prelude on an imaginary piano. I wanted him to do
everything he normally did when performing Bach except pro-
duce sound. His back straightened, his breathing evened out and
he began to play on the imaginary keyboard. His hands moved so
evenly that they could have balanced stacks of quarters.

When he finished, his body relaxed and his breath deepened. It
was as if he had temporarily become someone else. I called this state
his "Bach trance."

Next was imaginary Brahms. The audience watched him lean forward with a rounded back, breathe deeply and press his hands on
the invisible keys. Those hypothetical coins would have fallen off
this time. I called this his "Brahms trance."

When I asked what was going on inside him in each state, he said,
"In the Bach state I was counting, but not consciously. In the Brahms
I was feeling more and my body felt heavier."

Next I suggested he become Ravel. Again his breathing changed, and his fingers seemed to float over the keys as his body swayed slightly.

Finally I asked him to play the music of one composer while in the state of another—on the real piano. He laughed and said he'd try. He took time to prepare himself, looking at the keyboard and leaning forward with a rounded back. He played the Bach prelude, but I knew from his body that he was in the Brahms trance. Nothing could have prepared me for the shock this stylistic crossover produced. I was momentarily convinced that this Bach prelude was, in fact, written by Brahms.

The audience was just as surprised by the mix of music and style. We concluded that Bach and Brahms weren't so different after all— and that it was the performer who held the ultimate power over a piece of music. ❋

MIDNIGHT MARTINIS WITH HENRY BRANT

PAUL PRICE PHONED ME ONE NIGHT AND INVITED ME DOWN TO A fancy hotel bar near 6th Avenue and 53rd Street. He had just proposed to his girlfriend and wanted me to celebrate with him and his new fiancée. They already had a head start on martinis, so I jumped in and tried to catch up. I hadn't had supper yet, but they kept insisting I have another and another. Close to midnight Paul said, "Michael, you haven't met Henry Brant yet." I had played Brant's music with Paul at the University of Illinois, but it was true, I'd never met this icon of the New York *avant garde*. Oblivious of the hour, Paul phoned Brant, who invited us to his Greenwich Village apartment.

Brant and his wife answered the door in bathrobes, but cheerfully offered us drinks. I asked Brant about being a composer in New York. How could he support himself? By writing jingles and commercial arrangements for radio and television, he said. I was shocked and asked if he was serious. He said of course. I turned to his wife and asked whether their fireplace was real. She said it was. "Then," I told Brant, "I think you should build a big fire in there and take all your music"—here I made a sweeping, drunken gesture—"and chuck it right into the fireplace! Just chuck it!"

I don't remember seeing anyone's reaction, so intense was my state, but I felt a smile from Brant, who had a great sense of humor, and a chill from Paul, who cleared his throat and said it was about time for us to leave.

Henry and I became good friends after that and lived across the street from each other for several years. I admired his iconoclasm and was a fan of his work, especially *Ice Field*, for which he won a Pulitzer Prize in 2002 at age 89! ❋

THE RITE OF SPRING WITH CHIVAS REGAL

ON THE DAY IGOR STRAVINSKY CONDUCTED *THE RITE OF SPRING* for Columbia Records, he hobbled out of the control booth on a cane. Weakened by a stroke and a recent operation, he was facing one of the most energetic—and, for a conductor, physically demanding—compositions in the symphonic repertoire.

A sharp, young New Yorker named Robert Craft had led us through rehearsals just two days before, working out difficulties so Stravinsky could conduct *The Rite* in Carnegie Hall.

But a studio recording is different. Columbia producers wanted it to be a perfect record for all time.

Principal bassoonist Loren Glickman, the orchestra's contractor, called a group of us together. "Look fellas, this is a really important recording. The 'ole man'"—our affectionate term for Stravinsky—"could have a heart attack on the podium today. We've got to get this recording, no matter what. So whatever happens just play."

Almost every member of our 95-piece orchestra was a member of a string quartet or a brass or wind group, or was a soloist in his own right. I was picked to play miscellaneous percussion like tam-tam, gourd and antique cymbals. We had all pulled plenty of conductors through performances in our day, so we were confident enough to face almost any mishap on the podium.

The session started with Craft, then Stravinsky's assistant, leading a straight run-through, which the Columbia engineer taped in case they needed to cover a mistake. Then Stravinsky arrived on an assistant's arm.

He was in a particularly good mood and offered concertmaster Isadore Cohen—violinist of the Beaux Arts Trio—a shot of Chivas Regal scotch. When Cohen politely declined, Stravinsky looked around as if to say, "Anybody else?" Amid scattered murmurs of "No thank you, Maestro," someone near me muttered, "Oh my God..." Stravinsky, a scotch lover, was drinking to numb his considerable pain.

Timpanist Al Howard gave me a fasten-your-seatbelt glance as Stravinsky started off the opening bassoon solo with a smile and a gentle wave. He was never the world's greatest conductor but, as a seminal figure in music, he could inspire musicians just by his presence. We got through the slow and quiet opening section of mostly woodwinds. But when the tempo sped up, Stravinsky threw us all into shock with a simple move: he stopped conducting to lick his finger and turn the page!

We all went on alert. Principal flutist Sam Baron took his cues from cellist Bernie Greenhouse, who got signals from Cohen, who kept his eyes on principal trumpet Ted Weiss. These blasé New York musicians pulled together as I'd never seen in a group this size, hurtling forward like a Mack truck. The further Stravinsky strayed the more inspired we became. We were playing *The Rite of Spring* without a conductor!

At the climax, Stravinsky caught up with us, waving his hands with an exultant flourish as the piece thundered to a finish.

Afterward, we were still standing around talking about it. "You know, I feel like I'm a part of history," Glickman said. Little did he know. Scientist Carl Sagan later included our "Stravinsky Conducts

Stravinsky" performance in a satellite library launched into outer space. He considered it one of humanity's highpoints, Chivas Regal and all. ❋

THE ENCHANTED TRIANGLE

NOT ALL FREELANCE JOBS ARE GREAT MUSICAL EXPERIENCES— far from it. As a British cellist once told me about the music scene in London, "It's the same as everywhere else: the worse the music, the more you get paid."

The first jingle I ever played in New York was for the Chrysler Corporation. They booked the recording studio for one day and filled it with ad men from Madison Avenue. They needed only one musician and I was it. When I saw the music I couldn't believe my eyes: only one note—a single tap on a triangle! I thought it was joke, but the head execs were deadly serious.

Here's how the session went. First I'd play a "take" of my note, and the ad men would discuss whether the sound possessed the right character. I tried every kind of beater on that triangle. We constantly repositioned the microphones, fooling with recording ambience, echo, everything, but nothing seemed to satisfy them.

Finally, after several hours, a young executive emerged from the recording booth, hands massaging his neck, brow furrowed in thought. He said, "Imagine a white Chrysler—a beautiful woman steps out, and just then the sun shimmers off the hood of the car. *That's* your sound."

I looked at him, squinting my eyes and nodding, like I'd just had a revelation. Reaching into my briefcase, I pulled out another, larger triangle, handling it like a newborn baby. In a low voice I said, "I've never used this one before."

His eyes lit up. "That may be the one," he said.

On the next take I raised the triangle high in the air, struck it with an exaggerated arm motion and shook it a little to make it seem like it was shimmering.

"That's it!" he cried, "That's it! Hey, what's your name? I want to use you again."

I made more money that day than I usually made in a week. ❧

HARRY PARTCH:
IN THE NOSE OF A COW

THINK TWICE BEFORE INTRODUCING TWO COMPOSERS WHILE holding any expectations of the outcome.

John Huggler and I met in 1958 at the MacDowell Colony, where we were resident composers for the summer. We talked music and philosophy over beers at the end of the day, forging a friendship that lived on later in New York. Meanwhile, I was keeping up a correspondence with Harry Partch, famous as a fierce iconoclast who invented his own 43-tone scale and built instruments to play the music he wrote for it. I had gotten to know Harry when he invited me to Chicago to play in the recording of his *U.S. Highball*, a piece about a hobo's journey riding the rails across America in the Depression. Harry shared many of John's views on life and I thought the two should meet. I figured they would hit it off famously.

I scheduled the get-together for a summer evening at my West 75th Street bachelor walk-up. A fresh bottle of Glenfiddich waited on the table.

When Partch walked in and saw Huggler chatting in my kitchenette doorway, an immediate chill filled the room. I tried to warm things up with a few words about their views on music and life, but they eyed each other like two alley cats. I hardly had the scotch uncapped when they were hotly debating how composers ought to work. John argued that a composer had to draw on great music of the past. Harry said a composer was duty-bound to cut all ties with history. I nervously pitched in a few moderate ideas that they quickly tossed aside.

His veins bulging, Harry cried, "How do you know what it would be like to break from the past until you've tried it?"

John stood up. "Well, I've never fucked a pig but wouldn't have to do it to know I wouldn't like it."

"You haven't?" Harry said. "The best fuck I ever had was in the nose of a cow, because she licked my balls at the same time!"

Suddenly John was on the floor, rolling back and forth, laughing till he could hardly breathe. Harry was howling with that ho-ho laugh of his. I was stunned at first, then found myself laughing uncontrollably.

When the room finally settled down, we were exhausted. Harry said, "Now where's that bottle of scotch?"

And we talked like old friends until dawn. ❧

ROMANCING A SPY IN BUCHAREST

WHEN AMERICANS STARTED VENTURING BEHIND THE IRON CURtain on cultural exchanges in the 1960s, I traveled to Romania, Bulgaria and Russia on a hands-across-the-ocean goodwill tour with American Ballet Theatre. I was one of three "ringers" brought in to play jazzy solos with locally hired orchestras in pieces like Bernstein's *Fancy Free* and Copland's *Rodeo*.

Before we left, a US State Department representative urged us to be on our best behavior, reminding us that Romania was one of Eastern Europe's toughest communist dictatorships. He warned that individuals might approach us offering to buy personal belongings like cameras or watches. Such dealings were illegal in communist countries and could have serious consequences. Worst of all was selling transistor radios, because underground agents could use them in covert anti-government operations. He even told us to watch our conversations in hotel rooms, which might be bugged.

When our plane arrived in Bucharest, a man from the local musicians' union (yes, they have them too) told us that guild rules barred visitors from playing in their orchestras. That gave me the week off, a nice surprise after a demanding tour of Western Europe. With a

September sun shining down on us, trumpeter Fred Mills, violinist Jan Tomasov and I looked forward to seven days of complete relaxation.

Our hotel, a pre-war palace called The Lido, featured an outdoor wave-making pool lined with sun umbrellas, reclining chairs and ice coolers. That's where Fred and I spent our days reading and people-watching. We noticed a conspicuous group of sunbathers among the usual tourists. They seemed oddly well-fed and suntanned, luxuriating near the pool as if they were rich. But how could communist Romania have such a wealthy elite?

One morning I saw a bony, oily, sleazy little man in rumpled clothes walk in. Noticing us, he walked over and talked to me and Fred in German. I spoke enough to understand that he wanted to buy a radio.

He said his name was Johnny and he was a musician "just like" us.

"How does he know we're musicians?" asked Fred.

I didn't know. The guy reminded me of someone you might meet in a back alley selling "authentic diamonds." Naturally we weren't interested and I told him to go away.

A half hour later, a stunning blonde in a turquoise bikini joined the local "Miami Beach" crowd by the pool. She set up a reclining chair, but it collapsed and pinched her fingers when she tried to sit down. Helpful young man that I was, I grabbed a cloth napkin and ice from one of the coolers. Wrapping her hand in my improvised icepack, I made sympathetic sounds, trying to give her the impression that she was in the hands of an experienced doctor. I got her another chair, ordered her a drink, and went back to Fred feeling like a hero.

When the sun started to set, she walked by and thanked me in broken English. She said her name was Tanzy.

The next day she was back, reclining among the "beautiful people." She waved, pointing to a small bandage on her hand.

"What you need," Fred said, "is a translator."

Soon our friend Johnny reappeared and started in again about radios. "If there is anything I can do for you, just tell me," he said.

"Who's that woman?" I asked, pointing to Tanzy.

He walked over and talked to her for a few minutes. *"Geheimnis polizei,"* he said when he got back—"That whole group is secret police."

I didn't quite believe him, but all I really cared about was Tanzy. So I offered to look into radios if he could get me a date with her. He agreed and set a time to meet that night in a park near the hotel. He told me to come alone and walk around the park until Tanzy showed up. That way, if anyone was watching, our encounter wouldn't look planned.

That evening I strolled along the park's circular path until the bushes rustled. It was Johnny. "Just keep walking," he said, joining me. A few minutes later, Tanzy arrived and we all walked along "to make sure no one was following us." Then Johnny led us to a nearby restaurant for a dinner of pork chops, a delicacy on the menu. Our mishmash of Romanian and German made conversation awkward, but I gleaned that more plans were in store after dinner. Naturally, I paid the bill, and we grabbed a taxi outside.

It was getting late when we pulled up to a large, three-storey house on the dimly lit outskirts of Bucharest. Tanzy led us around to the back, where Johnny struck matches to light our way downstairs. We crossed a basement and climbed a circular staircase to a hallway with a door at the far end. Tanzy signaled us to stay put and knocked on the door's frosted glass panel. The door cracked open wide enough for her to talk to someone inside. Johnny turned to me: "You're my brother from Germany."

Behind the door was a small anteroom. Several men in their 30s, smoking and drinking in shirtsleeves, played cards at a round table under low-hanging lamps. A few others sat around talking on decrepit sofas. Tanzy pulled open a set of heavy soundproofed wooden doors and the room flooded with music that roared out of giant black market loudspeakers. All of the secret-police sunbathers were dancing.

The music was illegal of course, mostly American jazz taped from Voice of America and BBC London broadcasts and spliced together in fragments that had filtered through jammed signals. Ella Fitzgerald sang for a half minute, suddenly drowned out by Duke Ellington's band, cut short by Chubby Checker or Elvis. The dancers adjusted to the mood and tempo changes as if the music had been written that way.

As I stood in awe, a young man came over and said in English, "You don't like our women?"

I was surprised. "Of course I do."

"Then why don't you dance?"

"I really don't know how."

"An American who doesn't know how to dance?"

How could I explain that I was a musician who had always been onstage, rarely on the dance floor.

So I joined in. My clumsy dance steps struck them as something new, and they tried to imitate me. But I paid little attention as I drank and laughed, dancing with Tanzy and any woman who could handle my unpredictable feet. Johnny, Tanzy and I ended the evening at a late-night outdoor restaurant on the Danube for more drinks. I'm not sure how I got back to the hotel, but I awoke the next morning in my room alone.

A day or two later I gave Johnny the radio (Fred had one that was nearly worn out), and he arranged for Tanzy and me to meet at an abandoned freight car that her friends had converted into makeshift sleeping quarters for comrades avoiding the police. Tanzy spoke little English, but somehow we talked. Puzzled by her political alliances, I asked if she was communist.

"Sometimes," she said.

I didn't understand. "Are you a communist here?" And I tapped my head.

"No," she said.

"Are you a communist here?" placing my hand on my heart.

"No."

"Then where are you a communist?"

"Here!" she said, slapping her groin and laughing uproariously.

After that, there wasn't much left to talk about.

On the plane to Russia the next day, one of the dancers asked how I had enjoyed my week off. "Well, I met this slimy little guy who wanted to buy a radio. He introduced me to a beautiful blonde and I went to an underground night club with a bunch of spies…"

"Oh, you musicians are never serious," she said. "Forget I asked." ✴

DIPLOMACY BY VODKA

FIVE MUSICIANS AND A FEW COMPANY OFFICIALS LED AMERICAN Ballet Theatre's next mission behind the Iron Curtain into Moscow to round up an orchestra. We landed in the Moscow airport in cold, rainy fall weather, met by a coterie of Russian officials lined up on the airfield. They all looked grave—just what I expected from Russia. We shook hands formally on a red carpet and drove to our hotel for dinner.

As one Russian official stood to speak in the dining hall, a waiter filled our two-and-a-half-ounce glasses with a clear, white liquid that looked like glycerin. Only when our translators told us to down our glasses completely as a sign of good will did I realize they were filled with vodka. A light drinker, I could hardly face it. "I don't think I can do it," I whispered to trumpeter Fred Mills.

Without taking his eyes off the speaker, he muttered, "Ya gotta, man."

After some welcoming words, we all stood and raised our glasses in brotherhood and drank it right down. I felt a hot flash across my forehead that raced down my back and exploded near the base of my spine. I felt warm all over. I'd done it! But before food came, a second official stood up and our waiter filled our glasses again—to the brim. The first toast had been to America; now we were toasting Russia. We stood up and drank the second glass.

This time it went to my knees and elbows. I sat down and watched numbly as the waiter filled our glasses for a third speaker. Now we were toasting peace—well, who could say no to that? So down it went. With this round I didn't feel a thing—not even the glass in my hand. Then there was a fourth toast to something or other concerning the arts. Ten ounces of vodka on an empty stomach. The food finally came, with wine. And dessert with cognac.

The head of Gosconcert, the Kremlin's management office, announced after dinner: "Now we go discuss the orchestra." So we floated upstairs with liqueurs in hand. Fred and I smoked cigars with violinist Jan Tomasov while conductor Ken Schermerhorn and assistant conductor Yuri Krasnapolsky negotiated the number of Russian players we could take on tour. What we didn't know was that the Bolshoi Theater needed musicians for their own opera and ballet season, especially strings.

Yuri, who seemed to be the only sober person there, hurried over and said, "Hey you guys, they're talking Kenny out of our strings— we won't have enough for the tour."

In my state, this struck me as hilarious and I went over to Ken. "They're taking away all our strings," I told him.

"I know it," he said—and the Russians laughed and slapped us on the back, while Yuri sat down and cried. The next morning, hung over at rehearsal, we had the smallest third-rate ballet orchestra any of us had ever seen, and no one could remember how it happened.

Still, the tour to Leningrad, Kiev and Tbilisi drew big crowds that cheered the company and demanded encores. By the time we finished, we and our hosts had a fresh view of each other's countries— with no small thanks to that clear white liquid. ❋

Epiphany in Carnegie Tavern

THE DORIAN WIND QUINTET COMMISSIONED ME TO WRITE A PIECE in the early '60s for free. But they guaranteed to give it a string of performances on their upcoming tour. I was still earning my way by freelancing as a percussionist in New York and welcomed any opportunities to present my music to a bigger audience.

When I finished the piece, I asked Dorian's spokesman to pay for part of the copying costs. He said, "We don't have money for copying, but we're going to give your piece a lot of exposure."

A few weeks later I was having a sandwich and a beer in Carnegie Tavern. Back then it still had a pub-like atmosphere that drew musicians after performances. I happened to be sitting at a table behind Dorian's spokesman, and couldn't help overhearing him. He told a friend about the new down-filled, buffalo leather sofa he had imported from Sweden for his sun porch. If he had something that expensive on his porch, what did he put in his living room?

Obviously he could afford personal luxuries but wouldn't fork out a few dollars for copying a new piece. That was the turn-around. From then on, whenever anyone asked me for a piece of music, I thought, "I'm going to make sure they value my music as much as they would a sofa." I started asking for money and, surprise, people started paying me.

That night at Carnegie Tavern, my inner Business Manager was born. ✷

TURNING MY FATHER
AROUND

MY FATHER TRIED TO DISCOURAGE ME FROM A CAREER IN MUSIC because he was worried I would end up on street corners playing for change. He tried to interest me in studying at the Art Institute in Chicago to hone my drawing skills—not because he loved Picasso or high art. He just wanted me to cash in as a commercial artist. When I rejected the idea, he probed the music profession by talking to the barber in Chicago's Kimball Building while getting a haircut. (The barber knew the NBC studio musicians who went there for regular trims.) The barber said that studio jobs were coveted, lucrative positions. When my father told me about them, I shook my head. I had already begun my life as a creative artist. Playing commercial music was simply not appealing to me.

Dad made a last stab at changing my mind when he drove me to the university for my first semester in music school. "What will you do if you can't get a job in music?" he asked.

"I'll get one," I assured him.

"How many people make their living as jazz musicians?"

"Some do and I'll be one of them."

"How can you be sure?"

I had no answer for that one. After a long silence, I said, "Well, I might not be rich, but I'll be happy."

He was strangely quiet for the rest of the drive.

Four years later I graduated, was drafted into the Army, and then struggled as a percussion player in New York. I wrote about my life in letters home as jobs began to trickle in. I was especially proud of telling my father that the New York Philharmonic had selected me as their extra player. When the orchestra needed more than their basic four percussionists, I got first call.

"What's the New York Philharmonic?" Dad asked when I came home to visit. I tried to explain this was the top of the profession but he just looked at me. "Is it a steady job?"

When I said no, that ended the conversation.

I told him I was starting to get my pieces played.

"Where?" he asked.

"I just had one played at Cooper Union." I told him this was an art school that put on concerts. "They have a very good audience," I said.

He shook his head at my impracticality, hoping I would someday see the light.

That's how things went for my first few years in New York. Then a chance encounter changed everything. Dad was at a postmaster's convention in Pittsburgh, sitting by the hotel pool, when a colleague sat down to take in some sun. My father introduced himself. "I'm Michael Colgrass. Brookfield, Illinois."

The man looked surprised. "Are you related to Michael Colgrass the composer?"

My father was dumbfounded. To hear his son's name on the lips of a stranger was surprise enough, but from another postmaster! Was I possibly succeeding in my profession?

That broke the ice, but the real turning point came when I played in a Victor Borge orchestra at Lincoln Center. It was the hundredth anniversary of Lincoln's speech commemorating the end of slavery. Victor Borge! My father watched it on TV. When he heard I had spoken to Borge face-to-face, his eyes lit up.

I told him I'd walked over to Borge between rehearsals and asked if we were free for lunch.

Borge raised his eyebrows exaggeratedly and waved an arm toward the stage exit, proclaiming, "Go slave, you're free!"

Well, my father considered that the greatest event in my career. I was no longer an errant musician. The crowning touch was my inclusion in *Who's Who in America* and *Who's Who in the World*. The first thing listed in a *Who's Who* bio is the name of the subject's parents. My mother told me that after Dad retired, he would walk to the library to read my bio and see his name—Michael Clement Colgrass—in the opening line. The immigrant had finally landed.

My mother's attitude was different. She was unpretentious and uneducated, but intellectually curious, Irish to the core and able to laugh till she nearly fell off her chair. She never questioned my desire to be a musician. Nor was she visibly impressed by my accomplishments, including the Pulitzer Prize. She just took them in stride, nodding as if it were all a natural progression. And she was definitely not awed by celebrity.

I once watched her with the famous Louis C. Sudler—a statuesque businessman from Chicago—when my work, *Winds of Nagual*, won the Sudler International Wind Ensemble Competition. A group of us had dined in Chicago and posed for photos afterwards. My five-foot mother looked up at Sudler after the last shot and said matter-of-factly, "So what're ya up to now?" He laughed and draped an arm around her. Then he joined her for coffee.

I have envied Mozart and Beethoven, whose fathers gave them a leg up in the profession. But I had something equally valuable in my family—no musical interest from either parent, which left me free to shape my own life. ❉

MY CREATIVE DEMON

IN MY 50S I STARTED LOOKING AT MYSELF AS A COMMITTEE OF PARTS that carry out my thoughts and actions. I developed the idea from a Neuro-Linguistic Programming technique called "reframing." I was also inspired by the therapeutic approach of family worker Virginia Satir. She would ask clients to identify the part that was "complaining" and talk to it, even role-play its voice. NLP, a technique for modeling and developing excellence, took this idea a step further, identifying a so-called "Creative Part" and asking it for ideas on how to deal with the complaint. The Creative and Complaining Parts then negotiate a solution.

In fact I'd used a similar approach when having to figure things out for myself—especially when I was debating whether to be a percussionist or a composer. The percussionist in me said I shouldn't give up what I had spent almost a lifetime doing. The composer said my real desire was to write music.

I carried Satir's idea a little further and defined all the major parts of myself as if I were a whole production company creating my life. NLP cofounder John Grinder called my creative part The Demon after I told him that my composer part is a powerful force that needs to be harnessed. I recall saying, "The creative demon can wipe the floor with me if I don't keep him in check." Through John, I learned to utilize The Demon by making it chairman of the committee—all other parts work for this creative power.

I made a chart of my key parts: the Husband, Father, Business Manager, Provider, Jogger (my health part), Joker (who likes to play), Healer (who helps others) and Public Communicator (who tells the public about music), to name a few.

These parts came to life over the years as I needed them, so I gave each an actual birth date. The Jogger was born in my senior year in high school when I decided to run the school track every day, imitating a fellow athlete I admired. My Demon was born at age 10 when I saw Ray Bauduc play "Big Noise from Winnetka." The Husband was born when I got married in 1966, and the Father four years later when my son was born.

My Business Manager came to life on the night I described in *Epiphany in Carnegie Tavern*—and he almost immediately formed a strong alliance with The Demon. From that day on, they agreed not to let me start a new piece until the last detail of a contract was in place. The Demon had been burned too many times by starting a piece only to see a performer's commitment fade away. My Demon-Manager alliance grew into a coalition with The Provider when I got married—a triumvirate I call my Executive Staff. They operate completely on their own, telling me what I need to do and how and when to do it.

A case in point: when the New York Philharmonic wanted to commission me for *Déjà vu* for four percussion players and orchestra, my Business Manager pushed for more money and a better contract. The president and manager of the orchestra went back and forth with me until only one detail was left unresolved.

I was heading out the door on vacation with my wife and son, glad that this undecided detail would keep me from starting the piece until I came home. Then the phone rang. I glanced at Ulla with a look of should-I-or-shouldn't-I? Hesitating, I put down my suitcase and answered. It was Carlos Moseley, Philharmonic president. "Hello Michael," he said. "Just a quick call to say that we agree on that last point in the contract."

Before hanging up the phone, I heard the opening notes of *Déjà vu*.

I said, "Oh shit…" because I knew my quiet week of relaxation at the beach was doomed. I spent the whole time carrying around music paper, humming to myself, and saying "Huh?" whenever Ulla tried to tell me something. ❊

WISDOM BY CANDLELIGHT

ON A HOT NIGHT IN 1962 I WENT TO A SMALL GATHERING OF Tyrone Guthrie Theater members in Minneapolis with my then-girlfriend, actor Judith Doty. We sat on the screened-in porch drinking and telling stories with Zoe Caldwell, the host, and theater luminaries like Douglas Campbell, Michael Langham and Will Geer. I listened as they discussed the nature of theater.

Campbell pontificated rather grandly on the importance of developing craft, which he said too few actors took seriously. Langham gave a dissertation on putting together a theater production. Then came Will Geer, a special figure in American theater. He became known for his portrayal of Grampa Walton in the '70s TV series *The Waltons*, but he also appeared in movies and major Broadway productions of Shakespeare, Steinbeck and Blitzstein.

A veteran political activist with long hippie hair, Geer held down-to-earth views. When it was his turn, he stared at a candle that was the only light on the porch.

"Well, what is theater after all, but standing on the corner telling a story, and if you can make people stop long enough to pass the hat, you're an actor."

No one spoke. Leaves rustled in the yard. We waited for more, but Geer kept quiet.

Walking home, Judith was uncharacteristically quiet. When I asked what was wrong, she said, "Could I perform on a street corner and make people stop long enough to pass the hat?" I told her Geer was just making a metaphor. She gave me a long look and said, "No, he wasn't."

From then on I looked over each piece I wrote, searching for the smallest moment that might lose my interest, or keep the listener from staying until I passed the hat. ❋

COMPOSER IN DISGUISE

I SOMETIMES TIRE OF TELLING PEOPLE WHAT I DO FOR A LIVING. I SAY I'm a composer, and they ask, "What kind?" When I say classical music—symphonies, that sort of thing—their eyes glaze over as they find a way out of the conversation.

Sometimes my defense mechanism is to simply change my identity, especially effective at parties where people are desperate to impress each other.

One night my poet friend Jordan Deutsch invited me to just such an event. "Important theater people will be there," he said, which I took as a warning, but also a challenge. Sure enough, that night I found myself sitting on a sofa in a noisy room when a chic woman swiveled her cigarette holder at me. "So what do you do?" she asked.

"I'm a psychiatric consultant for Gimbel's Department Store."

"*Really,*" she said, her eyes widening. "But why Gimbel's?"

"Well, many of the young saleswomen employed there are the daughters of Eastern European immigrant families displaced by the war. Their fathers feel alienated in this new culture and suffer a loss of confidence, so these poor young women have a confused identity—one foot in the new country, another in their homeland. It's very disorienting."

She didn't even blink. She moved closer and poured out all of her problems, occasionally stopping to ask my advice. I would simply say, "How do you feel about that?" And she would dive into another dissertation on her childhood relationship to her parents and siblings. I would nod wisely. When I couldn't stand it any longer, I excused myself, saying I had an early morning at Gimbel's.

The next day, Jordan phoned me. "Michael, what did you say to Marlena last night?"

"Who's Marlena?"

"She wanted to know more about 'my fascinating guest.' When I asked her who, she described you and said, 'Your friend the psychiatrist.' I said, 'Psychiatrist! He's no psychiatrist. He's a musician!' She almost killed me."

It was a while before I assumed a false identity again, and I made sure not to get my friends in trouble. But I have dabbled in professions such as movie director (very big with young women), investor (harder to explain because of my clothes), and my favorite, "I'm afraid that's the one thing I can't tell you," which really raises eyebrows. "Let's just say . . . I solve problems."

Well, musically speaking that's true, isn't it? ❦

KENNY'S ANSWER
TO LIFE

KENNETH SCHERMERHORN WAS ALWAYS SEEKING AN "ANSWER TO life," something that would vastly improve his day-to-day existence. For a while the hunt focused on an "absolute" remedy to cure his insomnia. He did discover a few pills and herbs that helped on and off, but so far, no wonder drug.

We lived only a few blocks apart on the Upper West Side, and often engaged in long philosophical discussions looking for the Big Truth in life. One day he phoned me and said: "Mike! Watercress!" I asked what that meant. "Watercress! It's the answer! I've had water-cress with supper three nights in a row and I slept like a lamb!" I was surprised that centuries of philosophers and mystics had missed this, but I was happy for Ken.

A few weeks later I bumped into him on Broadway. He looked sallow and pale, shoulders slumped, as if he hadn't slept for days. I was happy to see him. "So, how's the watercress?" I asked.

"It doesn't work," he said. "I can't sleep."

Reflecting back on Ken, it strikes me that he was not looking for answers, but yearned for the discovery of something new, and then newer and newer still to excite him. He was like a kid in a playroom, fascinated by every fresh idea he could get his hands on. When one burned out, he was looking for the next.

Now Kenny has a concert hall in Nashville named after him, Schermerhorn Symphony Center—one idea that's meant to last. ❦

"I'M REALLY GLAD YOU WROTE THAT PIECE"

KEN SCHERMERHORN AND I SAT IN FRONT OF THE TV AND watched the premiere of Aaron Copland's *Connotations* at Lincoln Center in 1962.

Hearing a symphonic piece on television is a poor substitute for the real thing. It was especially bad in those days, when television sound was so primitive. Deeper instruments like basses and bassoons would disappear while piccolos and clarinets would scream out. I complained about the TV acoustics to Ken as the piece went on. But my real problem was with the piece itself.

Atonality didn't sound like a natural style for Copland. He was relying on his usual wide-open chords and spacious lines, but used dissonant instead of consonant intervals. The piece just didn't sound organic, and I found my criticisms intensifying as it went on.

The next day I continued my diatribe against Copland's attempt at 12-tone music as we walked down Broadway toward Philharmonic Hall. As we opened the stage door who should come out but Aaron Copland. He asked straightforwardly, "Did you hear my piece last night?" We felt numbed being cornered like that. "What did you think?" I cleared my throat and glanced at Ken, who looked down at his shoes. Copland was staring at me, his fellow composer.

"Uh," I said, "I'm really glad you wrote that piece. You could have written a crowd-pleaser for this opening at Lincoln Center, but you took a chance and wrote an atonal work, which set the tone for the future of new music at the Center."

Copland thanked me and went on his way. Ken looked my way: "Oh, boy—'I'm really glad you wrote that piece,'" he said, shaking his head.

I don't know if Copland saw through me or not, but I was ashamed of my disingenuousness. Having only spoken poorly of the piece, there wasn't a respectful thought in my head when Copland appeared at the stage door. From then on, I vowed to express my thoughts on any new work as if I were facing the composer— by starting with what's right about the piece and then pointing out where I think it went wrong, if it did. Any composer, me included, appreciates such close attention. ✻

BRUSHES WITH
LEONARD BERNSTEIN

I'VE WONDERED FOR YEARS WHY I NEVER GOT TO KNOW LEONARD
Bernstein. Our paths crossed many times and I could have taken
advantage of chances to forward my career, but never did.

I first met him at Tanglewood when I was only 20, about 15 years
his junior. I was talking to a friend on the lawn after playing a work
by a fellow student, Halim-El-Dabh, at a Monday night new music
concert. Bernstein, who had been in the audience, stood a few feet
away. He nodded to me with a smile: "Nice job."

"Thank you," I said, and returned to my conversation. In student
orchestra rehearsals we were used to the rather flamboyant Bernstein, who wore jeans, a vicuna sports coat, open suede sandals on
bare feet, and sported a cigarette holder. His fame was already well
established and he radiated the aura of a movie star, which he embel-
lished with an ingratiating manner that struck me as forced. So I felt
a tinge of embarrassment when he singled me out at Tanglewood.

Years later, when playing *West Side Story* on Broadway, I saw him
at one of the performances, standing in the aisle in a white overcoat.
He smiled, kissed his palm and waved at me in congratulations. I
waved back with a smile and left the orchestra pit.

About three years later I had written my first orchestra piece and wanted him to see it. I knew his assistant, Jack Gottlieb, who invited me to Bernstein's spacious home on the second floor of the venerable Osborne building kitty-corner from Carnegie Hall. We sat on leather furniture under high ceilings. My score was in hand. "Leave it with me and I'll put you on top of the pile," Jack said.

He opened a closet door, revealing a four-foot stack of scores, topped with a symphony by Walter Piston, one of America's most prominent composers at the time. Again I felt something was wrong. Why should I get ahead of others waiting in line just because I knew Jack? Besides, I wanted to show Bernstein the score myself. Called *Seventeen*, it was a wild piece and I felt he might miss the point if I didn't explain my intent. "I'm afraid that's impossible," Jack said, pointing to Bernstein's appointment book with a shrug. I thanked Jack but didn't leave my score.

I simply wanted a few minutes of Bernstein's time, as I knew composers had with Koussevitzky, Stokowski and Mitropoulos. To me, great conductors should be interested in living composers and champion their music, as Monteux had with Stravinsky. But more often major conductors seemed too busy, leading two or three orchestras and conducting only a few weeks at each. Many played certain pieces repeatedly, leaving the newer music to young conductors—a far cry from Koussevitzky, who conducted the Boston Symphony's entire 36-week season and continually searched for new music.

I next encountered Bernstein while rehearsing with the New York Philharmonic at CBS Studios for one of his famous Young People's Concerts for television. A score and LP of my *Variations for Four Drums and Viola* were stuffed in my bag. During a break I slipped into Bernstein's makeshift dressing room and propped my recording on a chair. I wrote him a note saying I'd like his response. I never heard back from him.

A year later I was mingling backstage at a New York Philharmonic afternoon concert. I was with my friend mezzo-soprano Shirley Verrett who was singing Mahler with Bernstein. As I milled around, Yuri Krasnapolsky, one of Bernstein's assistant conductors, walked over and said, "Hey, Mike, you know Lenny—come say hello." He ushered me by the arm and reintroduced us. Bernstein said dryly, "Still writing percussion music?"

"No, I've been branching out, writing for all instruments." From his expression—a signal Gottlieb confirmed later—I clearly should have gone through the proper channels with *Variations*.

Our final encounter was one that didn't happen: he never responded to my orchestral piece, *As Quiet As*. I did submit it properly, but Bernstein didn't see it because all concerts for the remainder of his tenure were booked.

Fortunately, other musical figures were more approachable. I spoke to Stokowski at length about percussion music after a rehearsal with the American Symphony Orchestra. Erich Leinsdorf, who performed *As Quiet As* extensively, discussed with me his idea of a Boston Symphony composer-in-residence. Aaron Copland sat down to look at my chamber piece, *Light Spirit*, and recommended me for my first Guggenheim. I always felt comfortable with these people. But there was a psychological or spiritual repellant that either Bernstein or I had sprayed on ourselves to ensure we would never connect. ❀

ABSINTHE-MINDED COMPOSER

ONE NIGHT I WAS RETURNING FROM EUROPE WHEN A CUSTOMS officer at Kennedy Airport pulled a bottle of Pernod from my bag. "Per-*nod*," he said, pronouncing the *d*. "You can't take that in. That's the stuff that eats artists' brains." I told him he was thinking of absinthe, but he shook his head. "Nope!"

His superior reluctantly came over. A harried-looking man, he looked at the bottle and said, "Pernod, that's okay," and hurried off.

Confused, the customs officer slowly handed me back the bottle. As I was closing my suitcase he said, "Hey, what'a you do?"

"I'm a composer," I said, and walked away. I glanced back and saw he was still squinting suspiciously at me, sure that I was getting away with something.

Customs officers remind me of music critics: you are at the mercy of the vagaries of their knowledge and moods. Will the premiere of your new piece get through unscathed or will you be accused of carrying a dangerous substance? Will the review be influenced by a family argument or a bad dinner? At least with a customs officer there is a boss you can turn to for a final judgment! ❧

FRANTIC ON
BROADWAY

WHEN I WAS PLAYING *WEST SIDE STORY* EIGHT SHOWS A WEEK ON Broadway, I always showed up well ahead of performance time. I would check the tunings on my drums and put my sticks in position for the quick changes I had to make. I also focused my thoughts on the music. There was a lot to think about: I played a number of solos and cued the stage manager with four loud "rim shots" to signal a complex set change for the famous dance hall scene. After the overture, I'd play a drum solo with my fingers to kick off the first scene. I had to stay sharp throughout.

One Saturday I was tired and went straight home after the matinee. I ate a light supper and lay down for a nap, setting the alarm to wake me for the 8:30 performance.

I woke up at 8:15. What had happened? Didn't the alarm go off? I grabbed my jacket and rushed out the door. I ran from my little apartment at 75th Street and Riverside Drive to Broadway. Running to the Wintergarden Theater at 50th Street would take about 20 minutes. I'd never make it. I hopped in a taxi and sat for an agonizing minute, realizing Saturday night theater traffic was too slow. I told the driver my predicament and he took 9th Avenue downtown, but cars were everywhere. As we inched along I was rehearsing my excuse for the fearsome conductor Max Goberman. "I had an accident." "My mother was sick." "The electricity in my apartment went off and short-circuited the alarm clock."

When the taxi reached 52nd Street, I paid the driver and ran to 50th, then two long city blocks to Broadway. I knew Broadway shows started at 8:40, with a 10-minute grace period to compensate for terrible Times Square traffic jams. As I sprinted around the corner to the 7th Avenue stage-door entrance, I continued my mental rehearsal: "I choked on a chicken bone." "I fainted from overwork." "I'm having a nervous breakdown."

I ran downstairs to the orchestra pit and heard the overture playing. I hurried to the pit entrance. A ladder led up to a trap door that opened to the pit floor. The door was closed and trombonist Arnie Fromm's chair was sitting on it. I knocked frantically and Arnie knocked back. As soon as the overture ended I heard his chair scrape and the trap door opened. I scooted up through it to my drums, just in time to play my solo that opens the show.

Goberman's eyes radiated fire, but I focused on playing the show. At intermission I knew the moment of reckoning had come. I left the pit and went to meet Max downstairs where the musicians gathered at intermission. He confronted me with arms crossed. His eyes were tiny red slits. "Speak," he said.

I considered my vast repertoire of excuses, but surprised myself by saying: "No excuse, and it will never happen again."

He was silent. "You said the only thing you could have said."

For the next week, I arrived at least an hour before showtime and made sure everyone saw me. ✳

BEN'S NAKED DEADLINE

NO COMPOSITION TEACHER INFLUENCED ME MORE THAN BEN WEBER, a roly-poly, good-humored New Yorker. Ben worked all night and slept all day, and left his one-bedroom Central Park apartment only to shop for groceries. He spoke with a slight lisp, his hands floating in the air much like Truman Capote's. He wrote music, taught private students and copied music professionally at home to make ends meet.

One of his biggest commissions came from the Ford Foundation in 1961, for pianist William Masselos and the New York Philharmonic. Ben had written for Masselos before, which is why the pianist picked him—and wanted only him.

Ben got a good start on the piece and said it looked like one of his best. He liked to write slowly, but was on a strict schedule this time and grew worried as the deadline loomed. The more he stressed, the slower he worked, until he finally hit a snag and had to stop. Only a few weeks were left now. After much soul-searching he called Masselos and said he couldn't finish in time. Masselos understood, but Ben would have to personally tell Masselos' manager, Herbert Barrett.

Shy and awkward, Ben tried to talk his way out of meeting Barrett—a titan among New York music managers. But Masselos said no. Barrett would want to hear his reasons. So Ben pulled his only suit out of mothballs and borrowed a tie. He struggled to sleep the night before the early-morning meeting. But he was ready when Masselos picked him up at his apartment and drove him downtown to Barrett's office at Columbia Artists on West 57th Street. Arriving early, Ben downed an extra cup of coffee and built up his courage.

Barrett greeted them cordially and showed Ben the signed photos on his wall from artists like Toscanini, Stokowski, Schwarzkopf, Callas and Ormandy. When the three settled into their seats, Barrett said, "So, gentlemen, to what do I owe the pleasure of this visit?"

Masselos looked at Ben. Ben cleared his throat. "Oh…we were just walking around downtown and I thought it would be nice to… come and see you."

"Well, great," Barrett said. "And how's Billy's piece coming?"

"Oh…fine, just fine." And they chatted about how much Ben was enjoying writing for Billy again.

"I couldn't do it," Ben told Masselos in the elevator. "When I saw those photos on the wall and looked at Barrett, I knew I had to finish the piece in time or I'd never live it down."

So he went home and made a pact with himself: every day he would go straight to the piano and write at least six full score pages before eating or dressing. He wouldn't even allow himself to sit down.

He did finish his *Concerto for Piano and Orchestra* in time. The *New York Times* described it as having "a surprise ending." In fact Ben finished it only days before the first rehearsal, when he probably just ran out of time!

Ben encouraged me to earn my living as a composer, which I have been doing for over 40 years. He showed me that a composer could survive by forgoing material things many of us take for granted. Ben had no steady job, no tenure or pension, but was happier and more secure than most people I've met.

Whenever I struggle with a deadline, I recall my mental image of rotund Ben standing naked at the keyboard, composing furiously and refusing to give up. ❋

THE GINGERMAN

AS A BACHELOR IN MY LATE 20S, I WAS THRILLED WHEN SEXUALLY explicit books by Henry Miller and Anaïs Nin were allowed in the country. I especially wanted to read the *Kama Sutra*, the Indian book on human sexuality that most Americans had only heard about.

I went straight to the section on aphrodisiacs. One of the key substances said to enhance sexual ardor was ginger, a food I had never tried—so I went straight to the supermarket at 74th and Broadway and bought some.

At home I examined this strange block, shaped like a bar of soap or resin, and puzzled over what to do with it. I certainly had no desire to eat the thing. I reread the *Kama Sutra*'s description, but hundreds of years of editors had apparently removed crucial details on application. I had a date that night and wanted to be the lover to end all lovers, Indian style. So I decided to apply it externally.

I rubbed the ginger block all over my manhood and waited for the enhanced Don Juan power to take effect. Within seconds, a searing-hot sensation consumed my gingered loins. I ran to the shower and stayed there most of the night. And on and off all weekend.

I had to cancel my date of course. I told her I had a family emergency—which was not too far from the truth. ❧

"Who Are You?"
Asked Elizabeth Taylor

One advantage of being a composer is that you can take your work wherever you go. One disadvantage is trying to concentrate when someone is talking to you. I might look like I'm paying attention but I'm usually preoccupied with whatever musical fantasy is playing in my head.

My wife once told me about a roof party in New York, but I wasn't paying attention until she said, "And the brick chimney collapsed and killed one of the guests."

That woke me up. "Chimney? What chimney?"

She cried, "You haven't heard a word I said!"

Since then, when she wants to make sure I'm listening, she just says, "And the chimney fell"—which rouses my attention. Not everyone knows that trick, and my lapses of attention have been legendary.

One night in 1964, my girlfriend Judith Doty took me backstage at the Lunt-Fontanne Theater on Broadway to meet Hume Cronyn, who was playing Polonius to Richard Burton's Hamlet. A small assemblage of actors was sitting in Cronyn's dressing room chatting after the show, including Cronyn's wife Jessica Tandy and film actor

Arthur Kennedy. Cronyn launched into a story about an onstage screw-up, holding everyone in rapt attention—except yours truly, who was floating a thousand miles away. Suddenly everyone laughed at Cronyn's punch line.

I asked him to repeat himself, which he did. But I still didn't get it and asked him to repeat the thing before that. Cronyn furrowed a brow at me as Judith fired scorching flames with her eyes. I coughed and made an excuse to slip out while they continued talking.

I killed some time walking around backstage. The stage itself was empty and eerily lit by a single bulb on a lampstand. I walked onstage and looked out at the empty seats like an actor about to address the audience. A woman behind me said, "Who are you?" I turned and saw a petite, dark-haired woman with purple eyes. It was Elizabeth Taylor. She was waiting for her husband to freshen up after playing Hamlet.

I told her I was a composer waiting for a friend. I had never thought much of her as an actress, but I was transfixed by her lavender eyes. She also impressed me as being rather selfless. She asked about my work and seemed genuinely interested, even though I was a complete stranger.

Soon Judith reappeared with some of the actors. As we grabbed our coats by the stage door, we saw Taylor and Burton just ahead of us. Suddenly the door swung open and a roar rushed in with a blinding light. Hundreds of fans struggled for a glimpse of the legendary couple. Arms thrashed out to touch a coat or rip off a button. Any of us could have been mauled. Judith, normally composed, recoiled, covering her face against the wall. Fascinated, I watched a phalanx of policemen hold back the crowd as Taylor and Burton lunged for their limo. Suddenly the car door slammed and they were waving from behind tinted glass.

For once I was shaken out of my composing state. After they drove off, Judith and I rode the subway home in stunned silence. ✷

THE ALMOST-NEVER-FINISHED CONCERTO

IN 1964 I STOPPED OFF IN BERLIN TO HELP ELLIOTT CARTER MOUNT his *Double Concerto* for harpsichord, piano and two orchestras. I had advised him on the percussion writing and he wanted me back to lead his percussionists through the German premiere.

Bruno Maderna was conducting. I knew of him as a central figure of the European *avant-garde*, a movement that was increasingly testing my patience. Composers like Karlheinz Stockhausen and Pierre Boulez had been pontificating like high priests of a new religion on how to write modern music, saying melody was dead, the future was atonal, and Europe was leading as American composers—except for Carter—lagged behind. As for Maderna, he approved the presence of a nonbeliever like me only because Carter had convinced him I could help.

Rehearsals were thick with Maderna's self-importance. I was viewed as an American curiosity and generally ignored. But on the podium, Maderna deferred to me. The reason, I gradually realized, was that he didn't understand Carter's very challenging piece. Rehearsals were not going well. Carter kept interrupting Maderna with instructions.

Maderna was most insecure about the last section, which ran two different tempos simultaneously, a test for the best of conductors. Clearly he was unprepared for it. He just flailed his arms around, hoping the musicians would keep up. And he kept his eyes on me to see when the piece would end: I played the last note, a single click on a pair of claves that signaled his misery was over.

To me, every percussion sound was significant—even a small triangle note. I would hold up the instrument, lean forward and play it out to the conductor. I was just as expressive with the claves. Maderna liked that so much that he actually leaned my way before the final note.

When performance time came, I couldn't resist a little fun. Near the final moments, I picked up the claves and leaned toward him as if about to play. Maderna's eyes widened and fixed on mine. I relaxed slightly, lowering the claves, and he went pale. I leaned in again, holding the claves high. His mouth opened as if he had stopped breathing. Suddenly I extended the claves and played the last note. Maderna sagged like a puppet whose strings had just been cut. Drenched in sweat, he mopped himself with a handkerchief and took his bow.

To this day I can see poor Bruno, still standing there, waiting for my final click. Who says you can't have fun with serious music? ❊

THE CAPTAIN'S FINAL MOVE

MY FRIEND BENT LYLLOFF HELPED ME FIND A BRIGHT AND SPACIOUS one-bedroom apartment when I stayed in Copenhagen on my first Guggenheim Fellowship in 1964. A ship captain was renting out the place before setting off on his next voyage. But his price was too high. So I negotiated.

I talked to the Captain's rental agent, who liked me because I was staying for a full eight months. That gave me some leverage. After much discussion over cigarettes and cinnamon pastries in her cramped office, we ended in a stalemate that the captain himself would have to resolve. She warned me that he was difficult.

When I saw him in the apartment, I was impressed. Six-foot-four, with thick ruddy skin, a long beard and an enormous beer belly, he had the eyes of a serpent, glassy and staring. His sea-faring uniform and captain's cap completed the effect. He opened two beers, lit a cigar and sat down to talk.

He relied mostly on the intimidating effect of his booming voice. But I saw through the bluster and held my ground. When we reached a standoff, I pulled two months' rent in cash out of my pocket and spread it out on the table. His expression changed—to a mix of frustration and fascination. Staring fiercely, he snatched up the bills and signed the papers.

I moved in a day later, after he had cleared out his clothes to make room. Finally—peace and quiet in my own furnished place. I walked around admiring the upright piano and hardwood floors.

I opened a bottle of wine and prepared *foie gras* and crackers. I toasted my negotiating skills and smiled at my memory of the Captain's face, clenched like a fist when he capitulated.

Before enjoying my snack, I went to the bathroom—where an enormous foot-long turd lay in the toilet. I grimaced and flushed, releasing a powerful gush of water. But it had no effect on this ominous projectile. I flushed again. Nothing.

I marched to the kitchen and pulled out a knife to cut the stool in half. But it didn't work—I had to hack through the damn thing with the serrated blade! Even then it didn't flush easily, so I cut it into quarters. Finally the water swept it down.

I walked back into the living room, where my *foie gras* had suddenly lost its appeal. Then I started to giggle. That bastard had the last word after all.

"I'M A SPY!"

THE COMMUNIST VOPOS POLICE WOKE ME UP AT MIDNIGHT.
I had slept through the East German border checkpoint on the train
from East Germany to Warsaw in 1964, without having my passport
stamped.

The police walked me across the railroad yard in the drizzling
rain, machine guns on their shoulders, into a shack where an officer sat at a small wooden table. He asked why my passport wasn't
stamped. When I explained, he reprimanded me for my negligence
and asked where I was going. "To a modern music festival in Warsaw." He asked about my profession. I said, "I'm a spy."

To me this was funny, knowing what an unlikely candidate I was for
espionage. But East German police considered everyone a potential spy,
and were not amused by my post-war American arrogance. The officer stared and said, very slowly, *"Ist kein spass"*—*This is no joke*. I told him
I was a composer, but he wanted to search my suitcase. A few sheets of
manuscript paper scribbled with musical ideas lay on top of my clothes.
"These could belong to anyone," he said. Now I was beginning to worry.

He rifled through my belongings. When he saw the mess of dirty
socks and old underwear and a few wrinkled shirts, he turned to me
and said, "You're a composer."

He marched me back along the tracks and put me back on the
train to Warsaw. ✳

WRITING A BALLET
OVERNIGHT

"ISN'T THAT A REMARKABLE THING?" SAID JOFFREY BALLET conductor Maurice Peress. "Two lawyers from the publishers of Ravel's piano concerto just walked in and grabbed the music right off the stands. We've got no music for Gerald Arpino's *Sea Shadow* tomorrow."

We were having lunch during a rehearsal break across from New York City Center.

But I hardly cared. I was preoccupied with surviving on two hours' sleep after a foolish night of drinking boilermakers with the London Symphony Orchestra's visiting percussionists. Paress went on to explain that Joffrey had been using Ravel's music illegally for years.

I surprised myself by saying, "Maybe we could improvise some impressionistic water sounds, since it's an underwater ballet."

Peress liked the idea and pitched it to Joffrey. Meanwhile, I managed to get through the evening performance on aspirins and vitamin B1. But instead of going home I met with Joffrey and choreographer Gerald Arpino at CBS studios to watch a film of the ballet.

When I saw how Ravel's score blended smoothly with Joffrey dancers Lisa Bradley and Richard Gain, I knew improvising was out of the question. "You'd need a new score," I said.

"Want to give it a try?" Joffrey asked.

"By tomorrow's matinee?"

His shrug said it all.

The new score would have to be ready by 12:30 today for rehearsal! It was now past midnight.

"Well," I said, "if you give me all the copyists I need as soon as I ask for them."

They sent me home with a movie projector at 1:10. I perched a clock on the edge of the piano and drew up a flow chart that laid out the key events in the dance—the turns, the dips, the scene where Richard and Lisa circle the stage. I kept the orchestra down to strings and a few woodwinds plus vibraphone to save time copying parts. I knew I could play the vibes myself to add spontaneous water sounds.

At 3:30 I phoned for copyists. The sun was rising when they started handing me pages to proof. By 10:15 we were out the door. A cab carried us to copyist Arnold Arnstein's place at 72nd St. and Broadway, where Arnie and his crew rushed the reproducing and binding of orchestral parts.

At 12:15 we left with the music—with 15 minutes to reach City Center, and no cabs going south on Broadway. I ran to the uptown side and threw my body in front of a taxi.

"What're you, crazy!"

"Emergency! 56th and Seventh Avenue, *now!*"

We pulled up to the theater stage door at 12:30. I ran down to the orchestra pit, where Maurice was conducting another ballet. He rolled his eyes when he saw me waving the score. He hadn't expected me to come through and, understandably, wasn't anxious to sight-read a new score in public in less than an hour.

I reassured the dancers that the tempo and counts were the same. All they had to do was focus on their routine. It was goof-proof.

The curtain was about to rise when production manager Jack Hartman tapped me on the shoulder. "Michael, I usually go out and announce when there's a change in the program. But this is different. It's not like we have a substitute dancer. I could go out and say, 'Today's performance of *Sea Shadow* will be danced to a new score by Michael Colgrass.' Or, I could just…say nothing. Of course it's completely up to you, Mike."

"Jack, I want you to announce that I wrote a new score for today's performance." And he did.

Dance critic Clive Barnes seemed confused in his *New York Times* review. "Gerald Arpino's *Sea Shadow* was performed again this past weekend and herewith hangs a strange tale." He had heard the ballet performed to Ravel only two days before, but called my score "an equally aqueous match." *The New Yorker* somehow picked up the story and said my music was "wholly appropriate and quite skillful…I can only say the Ravel score was not missed." I disagreed with both. Nothing could replace the slow movement of the *Piano Concerto in G Major.*

Now came the politics. My friend Ann Summers, an artist's manager in New York, called me up. "Michael, what's this I hear about your doing a new ballet for the Joffrey last night?"

I explained.

"Is this a joke? Are you kidding?"

"No."

"Are you getting any publicity out of this?"

"I hadn't thought about it."

"Modesty is fine, Mike, but you deserve a story on this." She advised me to call *Time, Newsweek,* the *Herald Tribune* and the *New York Times.* "I'm going to call them too," she said, "but you have to verify everything or it's just a second-hand story from me."

So I called the papers' dance departments and the *Times* music editor, Raymond Erickson. They were all interested. *Newsweek's* critic cried, "Oh boy, this is a whopper!"

Back at City Center, I told Jack Hartman about my calls. "But all publicity for the Joffrey company is supposed to go through Isadora Bennett," he said. "That's just policy."

Conscience-stricken, I called Bennett and came clean. "Oh, aren't you a dear for telling me this," she said. "Of course I'll have to kill the stories. This would be a tremendous embarrassment to the company." She had the story pulled from *Newsweek* and *Time* and the *Tribune*, but missed the *Times* because it went through the music editor. The dance world never knew because they rarely pay attention to music.

I charged the company a nominal fee for the score, with free use in perpetuity. Naïve of me, yes, but I wanted them to keep it in the repertory, which they did. After a few touch-ups requested by Arpino, the company played *Sea Shadow* for three more years—until Ravel's estate agreed to let them use the piano concerto again. ✳

"Who Is This Woman?"

I THOUGHT I WOULD NEVER GET MARRIED.

I knew some women idealized creativity and thought they could handle it. But when the pressure was on—when her parents and relatives questioned her way of life—she would push for traditional middle-class living. And that would interfere with my music. I had watched friends and colleagues gradually veer away from their dreams when they married and became breadwinners.

I met my wife Ulla at a recording session for a piece of mine in Copenhagen. Preoccupied, I didn't appreciate her at first. But I did notice that she was completely herself, with no airs and no desire to make an impression. She was a professional, writing publicity for artists.

I called her a few days later from a pub and asked if she wanted to join me for a beer. She said she didn't like bars and suggested I come to her apartment. Soon we were in her living room, having a beer.

I was immediately impressed by her intelligence and sense of humor. She was perceptive and had insights into people and events that surprised me. And she came from a family that valued artists, something new for me.

"So what's it like to be a composer in America?"

I laughed. "Well, you're not nearly as important as a doctor, a lawyer or especially a senator."

She knew America well from working as a guide at the UN and a reporter at several US newspapers. She said, "Oh, I think a composer is more important than a senator."

I laughed again. "You're just prejudiced because you like the arts."

"Oh, no. There will always be a senator from Illinois, but there won't always be a composer from Illinois."

That was a lightning flash. For the first time my creative part, instead of urging me to run away, said, "Who is this woman?"

She asked if I was hungry and offered to make dinner. A light bulb went off in my head—I had a chicken in the fridge! I ran downstairs, hailed a taxi to my apartment, grabbed the chicken and returned, feeling proud of myself. Seconds later, she emerged from the kitchen holding my prized poultry at arm's length. Apparently six weeks in my old-world icebox was a little too long. Fortunately Ulla had a fresh fish waiting to be cooked.

As I got to know Ulla, I invited her over to my apartment—a place that few had seen. She immediately offered to "straighten up a bit." I didn't think it needed straightening but said sure, go ahead. She emptied the closet of old shirts and socks piled on the floor. Several giant bags went straight to the cleaners. Then she vacuumed and dusted everything. I was so traumatized, I had to stay in bed for a day to recover. Or maybe I stayed there because I had no clothes.

After a few months, my Guggenheim ran out and I had to leave Denmark. We ate a last lunch at Ulla's cozy third-floor walk-up next to Strojet, Copenhagen's well-known walking street. I was being picked up by Bent Lylloff for the trip to the airport.

We said our goodbyes and I walked downstairs with my bag. On the second landing I felt as if a large hand was pressing against my chest, slowing me down. Tears came to my eyes as I struggled to keep going. Bent greeted me on the street and said, "Are you okay?" I told him I was fine and we drove to the airport.

For the big decisions in life I don't believe in weighing pros and cons. I think you feel the answer in your body, with an intelligence beyond consciousness. That's the sensation I felt walking down the stairs from her apartment.

Ulla and I corresponded for months before I invited her to New York to live with me. The problem was getting a green card. We both tried, but no luck. Then I sent her a telegram: "Let's stop this nonsense and get married." The Western Union woman who took the message read the telegram back to me in a strong Brooklyn accent. Then she said, *"That's* the way to do it!"

Ulla and I are still married 43 years later. ✳

(Left) An Irish-Italian union— the composer's parents, Ann Hand and Michael Colgrass, on their honeymoon in 1925.

(Right) "Fightin' Jack Colgrass", Michael's father, was undefeated in bantamweight as a professional boxer.

(Below) Colagrossi family members in San Marco gathering around bishop Feliciangelo, Michael's great uncle.

Michael Colgrass at age six in
Brookfield, Illinois.

Michael's first drum set when he had a band at age 11.

The teenager who made himself at home in Chicago's jazz clubs.

Experimenting with conventional life and sports at La Grange Junior College, Illinois. (Michael is left in front row.)

(Above) The composer as soloist in the premiere of his "Rhapsodic Fantasy" with the Danish Radio Orchestra performing in Tivoli Gardens, Copenhagen, 1964.

(Below) A surprise to all—with wife Ulla and son Neal in their country home in Hackettstown, New Jersey, 1971.

Colgrass uses his studies in dance and theatre in his workshops, as seen here in Fort Wayne, Indiana, 1972.

(Right) The composer writes poetry for his song cycle "New People" in England, 1967.

(Below) Colgrass tunes both body and mind for optimal performance, here in a workshop in Springfield, Mass. 1979.

(Above) Education and music for children are central to Colgrass' work. Here he prepares a college chorus for his "The Earth's a Baked Apple" in 1972.

(Left) Rehearsing with conductor Andrew Davis and violist Rivka Golani for his "Chaconne" in Toronto, 1984.

(Right) Colgrass gives performance workshops around the world and is a frequent guest at American universities.

(Left) Portrait by his close friend Heinke Brendler in Springfield, Mass. 1986.

Two American kindred spirits—Colgrass and composer Henry Brant— meet in Toronto, 2002.

(Above) The Canadian Arctic has been a great inspiration to Michael Colgrass.

(Below) The composer discusses jazz with his friend Paquito D'Rivera, the Cuban virtuoso.

PART III
1967–PRESENT

INCIDENT ON
WEST 57TH STREET

I PLAYED WITH MANY OF THE GREATS IN THE '50S AND '60S, FROM New York's best orchestras to the Bolshoi and Kirov ballets to the Modern Jazz Quartet, Dave Brubeck and Dizzy Gillespie.

I endured a lot of mundane gigs too, like commercials and film soundtracks, but I was thankful to be constantly working. Some days I played a rehearsal in the morning, concert in the afternoon, a ballet in the evening and a recording at midnight. Eventually I was working so much I almost slept in my dark suit, white shirt and long face (as the joke went in those days about the overworked freelance musician). But I didn't dare pass up jobs because contractors depended on me to be available. Besides, these gigs were subsidizing my composing.

One night, in the midst of my hectic existence, I was carrying my briefcase full of drumsticks and mallets along West 57th Street when I stopped and said, "Am I going to the concert or coming from the concert?" I checked my direction—I was walking west, away from Carnegie Hall, toward the subway, so I had to be heading home.

As I sat that night in my kitchenette, I wondered how I could play a concert with a great orchestra and forget it 10 minutes later.

I had become a professional automaton. I played, the audience applauded, I exited Carnegie Hall on West 56th Street—they on West 57th—and the whole thing was over by eleven to avoid the cost of overtime.

In fact, my life as a composer was hardly different. My pieces were being played for *avant-garde* audiences fixated mostly on musical fashion. Any desire in a composer to communicate was considered naïve. You were supposed to write "for yourself," never for an audience, unless that audience was an elite—namely other composers.

In short, I was growing stale with the success I had—just going through the motions. The thought of it left me numb, like a warning that my creativity would die if I didn't take action.

I spent the next few weeks writing down my thoughts. What came out was a string of satirical stories about the life of musicians in a big city: an insurance company offers a child piano prodigy a policy insuring his dream of success against damage, loss or theft; the Mafia invents a nonexistent opera star through fake publicity; the CIA sends an agent to investigate modern music concerts suspected of transmitting codes through the music, and eventually succeeds as an electronic composer; a psychiatrist decides that the best therapy for his hostile music-minded patient is to become a music critic. And so on.

Getting excited, I imagined these stories as comic theater pieces that performers could sing, mime, dance and act in a colorful and cartoonlike way. But I was a composer—what did I know about acting and dancing, unless I studied these arts firsthand? The thought alone was so invigorating I could hardly wait to start. And when I did, I could hardly stop.

Judith Doty directed me to Bill Hickey at the Hagen-Berghoff Studio in New York. I studied improvisation with Bill, a master of method acting, and became so enthralled that I signed up for a scene study course and wrote scenes for my partner and me. Next I took directing. Then mime. Then fencing and modern dance. I even donned leotards and finagled my way into classes taught by Nina Fonaroff, New York's best classical ballet teacher, by telling her I wanted to experience music from the dancer's perspective.

A new door opened when the Rockefeller Foundation invited me to interview for composer-in-residence with the Detroit Symphony Orchestra. I told them about my ongoing adventure in the performing arts and they gave me a generous one-year grant to study experimental theater in Europe.

Off I went to study with the Polish Tomachevsky Mime Company; new theater techniques and physical training with the Jerzy Grotowski Polish Theater Laboratory; and clown training with the Columbiani brothers, two crazy *Commedia dell'arte* mimes from Milan. They taught actors to dance on each other's feet, slap and be kicked, and fall off tables backwards onto a mat with someone sitting on their shoulders. Every morning started in the gym, where the Columbianis had us run and dive, one by one, onto a talcum-powdered tennis table, skid across it and somersault off the other side. That was "Good morning"!

When I finished my year abroad—and all the black and blue marks had faded—I was thinking less and feeling more, letting my emotions come through instead of holding them back. I looked at the instruments in my music as actors in a drama. I also became confident enough in my new, mime-inspired physical coordination to conduct my own pieces. Two of my satires became theater pieces that I produced and directed: *Virgil's Dream* (about a prodigy who became famous for not playing), and *Nightingale Inc.* (about the Mafia in the opera business).

I also visited schools to show children how to move their bodies to different styles of music, demonstrating my newfound movement techniques. And I accepted offers to lecture at universities, but only if music, theater and dance students would meet me wearing loose clothing, ready to learn by performing each other's arts. These "creativity workshops" became popular and attracted professionals from various fields. A salesman once told me, "When I go to make a cold call my hands are sweating on the wheel. These acting exercises are good for my nerves."

A software manager in one of my workshops asked me if I had heard of Neuro-Linguistic Programming. I answered with a blank look and he handed me a book, saying, "You already use a lot of this." He was right: like NLP teachers, I based my life on modeling human excellence, imitating people I admired. I visited the NLP training center in Santa Cruz, California, where I watched them study outstanding athletes, speakers and entrepreneurs. I became their model for creativity and studied with NLP cofounder John Grinder. Gradually I incorporated NLP techniques into my own "Excellence in Performance" workshops.

Through all of this I transformed my musical life and put away my drumsticks for good. I began seeing myself as a composer. Commissions came in as people realized I was serious. I spent my days at my Steinway, committed to composing full-time, do or die.

That was the real message from my confusion that night on West 57th Street. ❋

OPERA PICKLES

MY WIFE AND I WERE AT A PARTY OF LONDON'S MUSICAL DIGNITARIES in 1967 when we struck up a conversation with Dame Ursula Vaughn Williams, the sophisticated wife of Ralph Vaughn Williams. She asked about an opera I was writing and shared her thoughts on opera, trying to impress me by dropping names and a German phrase or two. She was quite the upper crust, but I was courteous, controlling my usual tendency to poke fun at such people.

Turning to Ulla, she said, "And you, Mrs. Colgrass, do you like opera?"

Ulla loves opera, but caught the dame's haughty tone. "Well, to me," she said sweetly, "opera is like one of those big kosher pickles. When I see it I think I want it all but after a few bites I have to put it down."

Lady Ursula suddenly looked as if she had choked on one of those pickles herself. With a polite *adieu*, she drifted off into the crowd. ✤

"I Thought He'd Never See It"

PEOPLE WHO HAVE MANAGED TO EDUCATE ME FOUND WAYS TO draw knowledge out of me rather than cram it into my head. They sensed that I had some hidden resources and showed me how to mine them.

My elementary school drama teacher, Gladys Hickes, would invite us to take the stage and do whatever we wanted—read a poem, tell a story or sing a song. I played my first drum solo in her class. She always smiled and applauded. She was endlessly patient. Of course she did pull my hair and shake a finger at me when I was rambunctious, but she showed me the value of creativity. (She also taught me the value of greasing my hair so she couldn't pull it, but that's another story.)

In my high school government class, students elected officers as our teacher La Rue Thompson sat in the back watching us run things ourselves. What an effect that had on me! He believed we could teach ourselves, so we did. He gave me confidence in my ability to learn.

Later, in New York, I saw impressive examples of how professionals applied the same principles that I had the luck to find in my hometown schools.

In the mid-'60s, a friend invited me to a rehearsal of Terrence McNally's comedy *Next*, starring James Coco. The play was about a middle-aged man who, through a bureaucratic blunder, is ordered to report to his draft board. I sat right behind director Elaine May as she talked to the actors. In one scene, Coco was standing in his underwear when a doctor—a bullish female sergeant—walked in to give him a physical. Wearing only boxer shorts, Coco covered his crotch with his hands, drawing a smile from the room but little else.

May said, "Jimmy, if you see anything around you that you can use to cover yourself, don't be afraid to use it." They ran the scene again. Still it was only mildly amusing. May repeated herself: "Use anything at all, Jim, anything..." On quick impulse Coco grabbed the American flag—standard decor in recruiting offices—and wrapped it around himself. As we all laughed, May said to a friend next to her, "I thought he'd never see it."

If she'd told him to use the flag, the gesture would have been mechanical; this way it was spontaneous. He now owned the gesture because she had allowed him to discover it.

In a theater directing course I took at the HB Studio, Romulus Linney showed us a variation on May's approach. He had each student direct two actors in a murder scene: a political assassin was creeping into a man's bedroom and stabbing him as he slept. A key point here was that the assassin had never killed before, but was elected to the job. Linney told us to make it dramatic enough for a first act curtain.

Yet it fell flat every time. Our extensive directions to the actors did little to help. Then Linney whispered a brief comment to each actor. They did the scene again—and it was hair-raising. What profound insight had Linney given them?

"You asked me to hold him down on the mattress," the assassin said.

"You told me to get up from the mattress," said the victim.

We laughed and applauded. It was an "ah-ha" moment for me. From then on, instead of giving musicians complex instructions to achieve a certain effect, I would suggest a simple action to make the desired outcome inevitable.

When Elaine Bonazzi sang my song cycle, *New People*, in 1975, I wanted her to perform one passage in a casual nightclub style. Being a classical singer, she was uncomfortable with it. So I told her to lean slightly on the piano—and her voice suddenly took on an intimate feel that worked perfectly. This simple gesture made the whole passage seem natural for her.

As I experienced early in life, the best learning comes from within. ✺

Eye-Opener from Joseph Heller

My friend Art Bloom's wife, Beverly, worked as a bunny at New York's Gaslight Club—a "gentleman's club" where waitresses served drinks in skimpy bunny costumes. She told me Joseph Heller was a member. His book *Catch-22* had just come out and I found it hilarious. I asked if she could set up a meeting for me. A few days later Bev told me Heller's reaction: "Is he gay?" She said no and he handed over his number.

We met for lunch at an East Side restaurant called The Italian Kitchen. He was an amiable man with smile lines around his eyes. We talked for a couple of hours about everything from living in America (the worst fate for an artist, he said), to the demands of creativity (he'd chopped off 200 manuscript pages of *Catch-22* at the behest of his editor), to salvaging a bad situation (his book was called *Catch-18* until Leon Uris came out with *Mila 18*), to how his success had affected his life ("Now I can get my teeth fixed"). We even had a surprise visit at our table from another author, Lillian Hellman, but I was too absorbed in Heller to really meet her.

One remark of Heller's stayed with me. He told me he wanted to hear my music sometime. I offered to leave him a ticket for a Boston

Symphony concert and he said: "How about we meet afterward and you can explain to me what I heard."

I laughed, but his words bothered me. Composers often assume that unappreciative listeners are uneducated, yet Heller was a sophisticated person who loved the arts—and still feared my music. What had we composers done to create such a gap between our work and smart audiences? That question has haunted me ever since. ✽

MYSTERIOUS PATHS TO
MUSICAL CAREERS

WHO HOLDS THE POWER IN CLASSICAL MUSIC? CONDUCTORS, managers, promoters, the press, performers, board members, record companies, the ticket-buying public—all are possible power brokers. A subtle combination of them all may decide which pieces get performed and by whom.

In 1965, the Fromm Foundation commissioned me to write a piece for Tanglewood's Festival Orchestra. I based it on an article in the *New York Times* about nine-year-olds who were asked to complete the sentence, "Let's be as quiet as…" I chose seven answers that inspired me, and called the piece *As Quiet As.*

Gunther Schuller conducted the premiere and the audience liked it, as did the reviewers. It was my most successful piece so far and I decided to make the most of it.

I wrote to conductors of the top 20 orchestras in North America, briefly explaining the piece and offering reviews and a perusal score. Of the 20, four asked for scores. One negative reply from the manager of the Brooklyn Philharmonic read: "When the next Beethoven arrives we will all know it, for he will be heralded by trumpets from on high." (Figure that one out!)

Of the four requests, all were rejected and two scores never returned. Leonard Bernstein's secretary at the New York Philharmonic wrote me not to send the score, because Bernstein had already programmed the concerts for his last two-and-a-half years there. Besides, he was now devoting his free time to composing scores, not reading them. The secretary added, "Being a composer yourself, I'm sure you will sympathize."

That did it. Coming in the wake of 19 other rejections, I took out my wrath on the 20th. I responded with a stern letter saying a music director's first responsibility is his job, part of which is looking at new scores. A few weeks later, orchestra president Carlos Moseley gave me a call. I admitted I was simply trying to get Bernstein's attention, but we still wrangled over the orchestra's submission policies. I complained that trying to contact Bernstein was like seeking audience with the Pope. He said, "Is it different with any other orchestra?" He had me there.

So my final tally was 0 for 20.

A few weeks later I got a surprise call from the Boston Symphony's librarian, who said *As Quiet As* had been scheduled for that season. Other performances would follow on a tour of major US cities. Could I send him the parts right away?

I was ecstatic, but puzzled: how had I penetrated the BSO's inner sanctum? I hadn't written Boston about *As Quiet As*, because I'd seen conductor Erich Leinsdorf at the Tanglewood premiere and expected he would have said something if he liked it. At any rate, after a successful tour of 13 cities, Leinsdorf recorded *As Quiet As* with the BSO on RCA Victor Red Label. I couldn't have been happier.

Naturally, other orchestras now wanted the piece too. William Smith, assistant conductor of the Philadelphia Orchestra, met me for coffee and said with a wry smile that Eugene Ormandy had just walked into his office. "He was carrying a copy of your *As Quiet As* record and told me, 'I just heard the most charming work, we must perform it.' I said, 'Maestro, we already did perform the work.' 'When?' 'I did it on last year's children's series.' He got annoyed and told me, 'Well it hasn't been done on the subscription series. We'll do it there!'"

Three years after its Tanglewood premiere, I went to a party of musical artists and patrons in Boston. The European hostess, a charming symphony board member and long-time contributor, was pleased to hear that *As Quiet As* was currently my most performed work. She leaned close to me: "You know, za night of za premiere I vent over zu Erich un' said, 'I like zat piece.'" She punched the air with a finger. "'I vant it performed in Boston!'"

I always admired e.e. cummings' words, "You, and you alone, create your fate and make your destiny." I would add that a little help from an influential board member doesn't hurt. ❋

BEING A COMPOSER FATHER

OUR SON NEAL WAS BORN THREE YEARS AFTER I HAD DECIDED TO make my living as a composer. I wondered how I could possibly write music and still be a good father. Peace and quiet were luxuries I'd taken for granted. Could that continue with a baby in the house?

My first surprise came the day Neal was born. A surge went through me when I saw him. My God, here was a human being totally dependent on me and Ulla for *everything*. All thought of composing fled my mind as The Provider took over.

Suddenly this new person was the main creative project. Ulla and I shared all duties, alternating nighttime shifts for diaper-changing and bottle-feeding. Always cheerful and imbued with super-human energy, Neal slept only two-and-a-half hours at a stretch in his first two years. Our heels dragged with sleep deprivation.

When I stole time to compose, I was so tired that my head dropped on the music paper. Yet, miraculously, I got work done. I was driven by need: a finished piece meant paying the bills.

What I hadn't expected was making a new friend. Neal and I played games before he could walk, kicking a ball back and forth from his jumper. He loved to laugh and invented ways to send us into fits of laughter. But there were also tears. One dramatic day in his "terrible twos," Ulla and I were scheduled to play tennis when

Neal began to wail. The babysitter was about to arrive. Ulla said, "We can't go. He won't stop crying. He just threw his toy in my face." She had a red mark on her cheek and I was furious. I knew a showdown was coming and this was it.

"We're playing tennis," I said. "Go outside and wait for me."

Neal was standing in his crib wailing at the top of his lungs. So I wailed back. With all the volume I could muster I yelled, "We're the bosses here, not you!"

He cried, "Aaaggghhhhh!"

I answered, "Aaaeeeiiigggghhhhh!!!"

Back and forth we went while Ulla covered her ears outside. Finally he sat down, exhausted, looking at me. When the babysitter came, he didn't make a sound.

That was a defining moment in our relationship with Neal. Now we had an understanding. He started asking when he wanted something and gave up the power plays. Still, he was willful and couldn't be ordered around. Fortunately, he was open to reason and learned to use it himself. Once, Ulla gave him a verbal lashing for locking the family cat inside a box. Unperturbed, he said, "You shouldn't get so mad. It can ruin your whole day."

When he was four, we needed to decide about his schooling. We were renting an apartment in Manhattan and owned a farmhouse in Hackettstown, New Jersey. The country schools were wrong for him and New York would restrict his freedom—we wanted him to explore on his own in a safe environment. So we looked around for a city we liked.

Boston was desirable except for the bussing riots. San Francisco was too far from New York. By chance we saw a TV segment on 60 Minutes about Toronto, a city with a broad cosmopolitan mix, first rate classical, jazz and ethnic musics, low crime rate, and a small-town feel with a two-million-plus population. We were charmed by Toronto, and eventually bought a house on a quiet street downtown.

We could now focus more on work, knowing that Neal could walk to school on his own, play in the street and enjoy the rich life of a stimulating city. The class photos at his excellent public school looked as diverse as the United Nations.

Every day I had a satisfying six to eight hours of composing. After that, Neal and I would play—foot races, swimming races, wrestling and football. He usually won, of course. Sometimes I would win and laud it over him. Then he would return with a vengeance and beat me and I would act confused, which made him howl with glee.

Very early Neal showed an interest in writing. This gave me the idea of showing him how adults make contracts. He wrote one which we both signed, stating that every day at 5:30 I "belonged to Neal Colgrass." We would role-play—he was Superman and I was a bad guy. Or he was Batman and I Robin, or the infamous Joker, whom he would always outsmart. I had developed a technique from my clown training of falling down the carpeted stairs in a controlled somersault, groaning from his latest punch. Ulla described our laughing and tearing through the house as a kindergarten out of control.

Neal was always interested in our work. Ulla once asked if he would prefer she stayed home instead of being a magazine editor, and he said, "No, I don't want a mom with dishpan hands."

When I started using Neuro-Linguistic Programming in my workshops, Neal asked about "this NLP stuff." I simply said it helped people focus on what they wanted and how to get it. I taught him that if someone said, "I don't know," he could ask, "What would you say if you did know?" A few days later, I was walking up to my third-floor studio when he begged me to pitch a baseball for him and his friends. "Neal," I said, "I've got so much work today I don't know when I could be free to play."

He said, "What would you say if you did know?"

"Uh…about 3:30, I guess."

"Great! See you then!" And off he ran.

My biggest thrill was seeing his confidence grow, a feeling as satisfying as any I ever had as a composer. Knowing I was helping him develop and enjoy life seemed the ultimate creative act. He is still our best friend and now lives in Los Angeles as a writer and editor. ✻

USE IT OR LOSE IT

FOR SEVERAL SUMMERS, I TAUGHT PERFORMANCE SKILLS TO MUSI-cians at the University of Akron. In weeklong workshops, I coaxed them through dozens of mental and physical exercises to help them play at their best. On the fifth day, they gave performances to show what they had—or had not—learned.

One cellist stood out by playing on the final day without an iota of improvement. She was out of tune, hands shaking, tempo uneven, notes fumbling. I asked what she thought of her performance.

"Not very good," she said. Did she know the music well? "Yes, definitely." I asked if she used any of the exercises I'd taught that week and she said no. I asked why. "I don't know," she said.

I told her to practice them offstage and come back out to per-form. This time she had color in her face. She performed with a warm vibrato, solid rhythm and strong bow control. I asked what she had learned and she said, "To prepare myself before I go onstage."

Hmm. Isn't that what the workshop was all about? Why did she have to be reminded? I was fascinated. When she said, "I don't know," she was admitting a mistake we are all prone to mak-ing: we learn something, enjoy its benefit, and then don't do it. Why? We don't know. There's something very human and touch-ing about this. ❧

"Stop, Thief!"

I WAS STANDING IN LINE AT THE CHEMICAL BANK ON BROADWAY when one of the tellers yelled, "Stop! Thief! Stop that man!"

A thin, nervous guy in a windbreaker raced past me and up 102nd Street carrying a large canvas bag. I don't know what possessed me, but I took off after him. Maybe I was mad that I had to stand in line to cash a $25 check while he just took the money and ran. Maybe I had seen too many macho movies. At any rate, I was soon chasing him down West 103rd toward Riverside Park, yelling, "Po-lice! Stop that man. Po-*liiice!*"

Two students heard the urgency in my voice and darted out of a brownstone to join the chase. We followed the robber down the steps into Riverside Park as he jumped the wall. He cut diagonally toward the busy Hudson parkway, limping from the jump. I kept up my cry, "Po-*lice!* Stop that man!" Two joggers joined in and filled out our posse to five. With each of my operatic outbursts I noticed the robber flinch. From the sound he might have thought he was being chased by a linebacker from the New York Giants.

We chased him across the parkway as car horns honked and drivers cursed. The robber hesitated on the thin grassy strip between the highway and the Hudson River. "Give it up, man!" I yelled. "There's no place to go." He slumped to a sitting position on the grass, gasping for breath and looking at me. A police car pulled up and two cops dragged his sagging body to the car.

I talked excitedly with my fellow runners as we walked back to the bank. Inside, I hurried to the head of the line and told the teller, "We got him!"

"I know," he said. "We heard it on the radio. Get back in line."

I walked into the manager's office and told him everything. "Oh, you're the guy who was chasing him!" he said. "We'll have a reward for you." He promised to call later on. When he did, his tone was apologetic. "I'm sorry to say the reward is only $100. Our policy is to give a percentage of the recovered money, but apparently he was throwing money away as he ran. On top of the $100, though, we will give you a lifetime interest-free checking account."

It struck me that I could have just stopped and picked up the money the robber was throwing away.

The New York Times ran the story on December 17th, Beethoven's 200th birthday, along with a poem I dedicated to him. It was addressed "Dear Beethoven":

> *To honor your bicentenary*
> *I want to write a great piece*
> *But what could I compose for you*
> *Who grabbed the throat of destiny*
> *And spat in the eye of kings?*
> *We have no dragons to defeat*
> *So I did the next best thing*
> *I went out and caught you a thief*
> *Happy Birthday L.v.B.*

My father called when he read the story in the local paper. "Are you crazy? What if he had a gun?"

"I knew he didn't," I said.

"How did you know?"

"Because he didn't use it."

After moving to Toronto, I often visited New York but rarely used the Chemical Bank. One day I walked into the 102nd Street branch, introduced myself to the new manager and said I wanted to check my balance. I took pride in the account always being there. He searched the files and said it had been closed. I told him it was a lifetime free account for catching a bank robber. "The account's inactive," he said.

Cool, detached, indifferent—welcome to the world of banking. ✳

DANNY KAYE'S
NOODLE TREE

NOODLES GROW ON TREES. THAT'S WHAT DANNY KAYE TOLD THE petite Olga Koussevitzky as he bounced her on his knee.

I caught this charming moment at a fundraiser for Youth Concerts at Symphony Hall for the Boston Symphony Orchestra in 1975. A piece of mine called *The Earth's a Baked Apple* for high school chorus and orchestra, which the BSO had commissioned, was featured on the concert. Danny Kaye used his comedic talents, cutting up as a conductor with the orchestra in a hilarious performance of famous orchestral excerpts.

At a break during morning rehearsal, I was chatting with Danny Kaye in the green room when in walks Olga Koussevitzky, widow of the renowned conductor. Except for her trim black suit, she looked almost like a child at 4 feet 10 inches and 90 pounds. Bubbling with enthusiasm, she cried, "Danny!" as he picked her up and put her on his knee like a favorite child.

"What are we doing today?" she asked, wide-eyed.

"After tonight's concert we're going to have special Chinese noodles."

"How are they special?" she asked.

"They grow on noodle trees."

"Noodles don't grow on trees."

"Of course they do, same as spaghetti."

He went on to tell her how spaghetti was grown and harvested, and she savored every word until he explained how they imported special pasta pickers to remove the wiggling strands from trees while they were still wet. At this point she beat her little fists on his chest and howled with laughter.

After the concert, he was the cheerful pied piper taking a group of us to his favorite Boston Chinese restaurant. Kaye was a connoisseur of Chinese food and even had a kitchen built for it in his house. At one point, he led our entire party to the restaurant kitchen to applaud the cook, who turned a lump of dough into strands of thin noodles in minutes by smacking them on a board with the sound of a shotgun.

Excitement and laughter seemed to surround Kaye everywhere. But most memorable for me that evening was my conversation with Graham Kerr, known in those days as the Galloping Gourmet. He cooked elaborate dinners on TV in an authoritative style.

We sat next to each other, but my friendly efforts to chat were met with a cold and unresponsive attitude. His arrogance inspired the devil in me. I waited till we started eating.

"You're in luck tonight, sitting next to a man who makes the world's best spaghetti sauce," I said. "And I'll let you in on my secret."

He looked at me like something crawling on his arm.

"The secret is pork, but I'll get to that in a minute."

He scanned the table, probably looking for another empty seat.

"Get the best quality tomatoes and skin them to take out the bitterness. The easiest way to do that is to heat each tomato over a flame, which loosens the skin. Maybe you knew that."

He grimaced.

"Then add a can of tomato paste to thicken the sauce, and lots of garlic and oregano. Now, the crowning touch." (Did I hear a slight moan?) "Sear the pork chops on both sides in lots of olive oil. To give the sauce a nice brownish color, scrape the frying pan and add the remnants of burned meat to the sauce along with the chops."

Without a word, he stood up, looked wanly at his Peking duck and noodles, and left the table. That was the last I saw of him, until one day I caught him on TV. He was demonstrating what he called a "delicate sauce," but didn't use any of my advice. ❇

HIT BY PULITZER
BUCKSHOT

I WAS DIRECTING MY CHILDREN'S OPERA, *SOMETHING'S GONNA HAPPEN*, in my son's school in Toronto when I was called to the principal's office to answer a phone call. My first thought was of some emergency at home.

I picked up the principal's phone and heard the eager voice of an AP reporter. He sounded new on the job.

"Mr. Colgrass," he said, "did you know you just won the Pulitzer Prize for your orchestra piece, *Déjà vu?*" When I told him I didn't know, he said, "You mean I'm the first one to tell you?" He was thrilled to be the bearer of great tidings. "Well, would you tell me, right off the top of your head, your spontaneous response to this news?"

I thought a minute. "To me prizes are like buckshot. They might hit anyone standing in the vicinity."

Dead silence.

"But...but, aren't you pleased?"

Still looking for spontaneity, I said, "Well, my parents will be pleased, especially my father."

He was crestfallen. I was beginning to feel bad for him. "Yes, I'm very pleased," I said.

My feelings were mixed. I knew the prize would raise my stock in the music world, but at the same time I was aware that—unlike an athletic event where you have a clear winner—the winner of the Pulitzer Prize is chosen by a few people. Change one person on the jury and the prize would likely go to another composer whose work is as good or maybe better.

Perhaps the biggest pleasure for me was knowing that those who believed in me could have their opinion "officially" confirmed. For a couple of days my phone kept ringing as friends and neighbors came by with champagne. It was like a birthday party.

Then it was back to work, and the only thing that mattered was my next piece. ❋

Dizzy's Magnetic Head

DIZZY GILLESPIE REALLY WAS DIZZY. OR SO I LEARNED ONE DAY AT Anna Kalso's apartment in Toronto.

Anna was known in the '70s for creating the Earth Shoe, an oddly shaped thing designed to balance the body. I found them rather uncomfortable, but loved Anna for her joyful eccentricities.

Her lively parties had an eclectic mix of people. At one, I saw Gillespie for the first time in 10 years (I had played with his band on a recording conducted by Gunther Schuller in the '60s). True to form, Anna pulled out a pendant on a silver chain and held it over each person's head, to demonstrate their "inner magnetism." Over one head it rotated clockwise, over another counterclockwise, or back and forth in a consistent pattern.

Then she got to Dizzy. The pendant swung gently from side to side, then spun clockwise, then counterclockwise and suddenly jerked away in jagged motions. It simply would not hold to one pattern. We all laughed.

"Now we know how you got your nickname, John," Anna said.

But Dizzy wasn't mentally dizzy. He was a sharp observer. As we traded stories about musicians, he told one about tenor sax great Stan Getz. One night after a gig, putting his instrument in the trunk of a car, Getz said, "I'll never be a great jazz musician because I'm not black."

Here Gillespie scowled in disgust. "Oh, bullshit!" he told him.

I liked Gillespie's response. Instead of going into a long discussion of history and genes, he summarily dismissed Getz's self-deprecating attitude. If only more American and Canadian composers were so confident when told they can't compose music as well as Europeans.

But is this lack of confidence always sincere? Finishing his story, Dizzy leaned over to me: "He was just fishing for a compliment." ❧

FLOATING DOWN
THE ROOT CANAL

JAZZ HORN PLAYER BERNIE PILTCH TOLD ME HE'D UNDERGONE extensive dental treatment without anesthetic. Allergic to Novocain, he used what he called "hypnosis therapy." I asked if he felt anything when the dentist drilled. "You feel it but you don't care," he said.

Fascinated, I signed on for pain control sessions with Bernie's hypnotherapist in Toronto, Dr. Susan Schulman.

I had no idea if this would work for me, and I was suspicious after having taken part in a stage hypnotist's act with my band as a teenager. The hypnotist used the "count-backwards-from-10" approach while swinging a pocket watch in front of our eyes to induce a trance. That seemed to work on our trombone player, whose body became suspended like a board between two chairs as the hypnotist walked on him. My mother recalls that I winked at her while I was supposed to be in a trance, which probably disqualified me as a good subject. So it was with mixed feelings that I visited Dr. Schulman.

Her approach was much subtler than what I had seen in stage hypnotists. Her voice soothed me in the comfortable chair, but dialogue swirled in my head, fighting my innate skepticism. Just when I was about to tell her this wasn't working, I noticed my left hand rise in the air all by itself. I wasn't asleep, so I was puzzled.

Then I found myself sitting by a fireplace in an Arctic lodge as icy winds blew outside. She told me to warm my hands by the fire. Walk to a window. Place my fingers against the frozen glass. Go back to the fire.

Soon I was putting on a fur coat, hat and gloves, and walking out in the swirling snow. She asked me to take off a glove, plunge my hand into the snow and rub some on my jaw to freeze my face. Then back to the lodge, heavy clothes off and hands warming by the fire again.

When I awoke she told me to visit the lodge again before going to the dentist.

At my next dental checkup, Dr. Balinsky told me with cheerful professionalism that I had an abscessed molar needing a root canal right away. As he reached for the Novocain, I told him I'd rather go without it. His cheerful demeanor faded. He assured me that freezing was necessary. I reassured him I'd be okay. I had no idea if I was truly ready, but I felt I had to try out my new skills.

I asked for a minute while I plunged my whole face in the snow outside my secret northern lodge, then signaled him to start. As my muscles let go I began to sink heavily into the chair. I felt like I was outside my body watching myself.

Dr. Balinsky drilled into the filling on the top of the molar. I heard him grunt a few times as if it weren't working. I mumbled, "What's the matter?"

"I can't find the nerve," he said. "It's calcified."

I told him I'd signal as he got closer. I could feel faint sensations when he approached the nerve. Suddenly I knew he had found it and mumbled, "'ull's ay."

"What?" he said.

"Bull's eye!"

After he finished, his dental assistant said, "I never saw anyone do that before."

I didn't tell her it was my first time. I had read about people using hypnosis and Mesmerism in various forms as an anesthetic in the 19th Century. Sometimes ether, opium or cocaine were unavailable, or were rejected for religious or moral reasons.

I have hypnotized myself at the dentist many times since my first try, and I always find it refreshing to walk out without a frozen face. I suffer no pain, bleeding or swelling, and I don't need to take the painkillers. I love to treat myself, though, to a heaping portion of gelato. ❋

THE ESSENCE OF HYPNOSIS

WRITING ABOUT SELF-HYPNOSIS TAKES ME BACK TO GEORGE Faludy, Hungary's national poet, whom I met when Ulla interviewed him in the late '80s. We sat in our living room in Toronto on the coldest February day I can remember—the sort of cold that makes icicles in your nose. People were bundled up in hooded parkas and heavy boots to navigate the frozen snow. But when Faludy walked up our front steps, he wore only a light coat, sandals and no socks!

During a break in Ulla's interview, I asked about his spring attire. He said he had Albert Einstein to thank for it.

In 1950, the scientist told him never to wear socks, because they cut off circulation to the feet. He also recommended not to cut his hair. I don't know what the health benefits were of that advice, but Faludy's head was a wild bush that hadn't seen scissors in years. I asked if he didn't get cold and he shook his head. From the moment he followed Einstein's advice, he never felt cold in winter.

I asked why he decided to take such strange counsel, and he said, "Well, he was Einstein."

Faludy's experience is a perfect example of self-hypnosis. Believe something hard enough and your psyche makes it so. Often your belief comes from trust in the person who offers the idea.

I think Carl Jung would agree. In *Memories, Dreams, Reflections,* he writes about the first time he used hypnosis. He made an appointment with a woman on crutches who had been suffering from severe leg pain for 17 years. A group of 20 students were invited to watch. This middle-aged woman, who had a strong religious bent, expressed her great admiration for Jung and her confidence that he would cure her. She was so assured of his powers that the very moment he described his plan to hypnotize her she dropped spontaneously into a trance, all by herself. Jung was alarmed and confused, especially when he couldn't awaken her. Naturally he feared something was wrong and felt embarrassed in front of his students. After a short while she awoke on her own, stood up, threw aside her crutches, and cried "I'm cured!"

Jung was so shaken that he abandoned hypnosis altogether, knowing there was much he didn't understand. A year later, the same woman came to him again, complaining of back pain. As he asked her about it, she fell into a deep trance on her own. When she awoke she said the pain was gone.

He never figured out what had happened. But I think it's obvious that she had such a strong faith in Jung—as did Faludy in Einstein—that his very presence was enough to bring out her own natural healing powers. ✳

VIOLINISTS AND FOOTBALL

ITZHAK PERLMAN ONCE TOLD ME HOW MUCH HE LOVED WATCH-ing basketball. He especially enjoyed seeing the ball go into the basket without touching the rim (called a "swisher") because he said that was like hitting a note exactly in tune—right in the center.

His remark inspired me to give a workshop at the University of New Mexico for athletes and musicians. I wanted to see what we could learn about the relationship between two such seemingly disparate skills.

I showed them exercises for managing their states of mind to get the best performance. In the first hour I noticed a violinist glancing disdainfully at a giant football player beside her. As the day went on, her scowl intensified. I wondered if she considered athletes beneath her.

At one point, I thought it was time for a demonstration in performance. I asked Aaron, a wiry, intense wide receiver on the college football team, to step up and tell us what goes through his mind before he runs out to catch a pass. At first he was speechless, unused to talking about it, but my questions sparked a few words.

"I see all the guys on the other team, and I map my route so I can fool the defenders and still get where I'm supposed to be," he said, pointing across the room. "Then I feel myself running toward that position while I'm watching the ball in the air, so the ball and I can meet at the same place."

A few chuckled in appreciation of his obvious good sense.

"Anything else?" I asked.

"Yeah. Now I'm there, and I'm thinking, 'Don't run 'til you feel the ball in your hands'—we can make that mistake, turning to run before we catch it, because we're afraid of getting hit."

I asked him to go through the whole mental process of catching the ball while standing in place. His eyes glazed over and his facial muscles slackened. He looked up as his hands clamped together and drew quickly into his chest, his torso dipping and turning away.

"How did it go?" I said.

"Good."

"Did you catch it?"

"Definitely."

"How do you know?"

"Because I can feel it."

This really caught the violinist's attention. "That's amazing," she said. "That's exactly what I do before I play. I hear the whole performance and I feel it happening. And then I step into the part. But I think it would help to not just hear it first, but also *see* it the way Aaron does."

She joined in a round of applause as he sat back down.

So when someone says, "That person's very intelligent," I ask, "What kind of intelligence?" I think everyone is a genius at something, although the smartest among us are capable of doing some of the dumbest things. ❋

"What's the Matter— Can't You Count?"

Speaking about physical intelligence and coordination, some of the brightest people don't have it. For them, synchronizing the fingers with the brain when playing rhythms can be a big challenge.

Manny Vardi told me that when he, Isadore Cohen and Bernie Greenhouse gave trio concerts near Princeton they would often drop in on Albert Einstein and invite him to play second violin as they read through some simple quartets. Einstein was not in their class of course, but he was a lot of fun to be with and loved trying to play with these great musicians.

They had an ongoing joke about Einstein's shaky sense of rhythm. When he lost his way, one of them would say, "No, no, no, Albert. One-two-three-four—what's the matter with you, can't you count?"

Manny said Einstein would laugh the loudest. ❧

Appreciation by Proxy

I was sitting in a box seat at New York's Tully Hall one night when someone tapped me on the shoulder. I turned around to face a cheerful man with twinkling eyes. "Hi, I'm Barry Tuckwell," he said. I knew of him as the Australian horn player in the society's chamber group. Before I could introduce myself, the lights went down and the concert began.

Tuckwell picked up our conversation at intermission. "I have to catch a flight so I'm not staying for the rest," he said. "But I just wanted to tell you how much I like your music. You're rare among composers today. Your music is fresh, lyrical and rhythmically exciting. You know how to make modern music sing."

I thanked him and said I appreciated his remarks.

He shook my hand. "I couldn't leave without telling you that. Goodbye, Mr. Bolcom."

William Bolcom is a composer with hair and complexion much like mine. I haven't seen Mr. Tuckwell since, but I wondered if I should introduce myself if I do. ✳

PSYCHIC FEATHERS

IN A CONFERENCE CENTER IN MONTEREY, CALIFORNIA, A GROUP OF Neuro-Linguistic programmers asked how I write music, whether I see it in my head, feel the notes going by, or even smell them as pass. This was a typical "modeling" session under the guidance of NLP cofounder John Grinder.

Discussing creativity, I told them about a teenage girl who auditioned well for a musical play of mine but demurred when I asked her to dance. With her long limbs and graceful manner, I thought she would be a natural dancer. So I pointed to my empty hand and said, "See that feather?" The other kids waiting around looked at me like I was crazy. I opened her hand and placed the imaginary feather on her palm. "Now, whatever you do, don't drop it," I said, and put on a tape of the beautiful slow movement of Mozart's *Piano Concerto No. 14 in Eb*.

Inspired by the music, she walked across the stage testing the lightness of the feather. She dipped her body this way and that and turned in circles, balancing the imaginary feather on her flat hand. Gaining confidence, she raised her hand high in the air—palm up of course—and turned in circles. She finished with a flourish and disappeared into the wings. The scene was so magical, the other students applauded. She said afterwards, "May I keep the feather?"

At this point, the NLP modelers stopped flooding me with questions about composing and asked me to move around as the girl had, balancing an imaginary feather in my hand.

"Imagine that the feather is not there," said one.

"Now see it growing in size," said another.

"Now shrinking..."

"Now changing color...

My head was swirling with these images as I did my best to carry out their instructions, dancing without music. Then someone said, "Close your eyes."

I did, standing still. Another asked me to describe the feather I was seeing in my mind's eye. It had looked small and white, like the feather of a seagull, but now appeared as a long, purple plume.

"Open your eyes!" another trainer cried.

I did. Right on the floor in front of me was a lady's hat with a long purple feather. "Damn!" said Grinder. He wanted to see what would have developed if I had kept going with my eyes closed.

The far wall of the convention center suddenly looked different to me. Instead of the gray curtain that hung there, I saw the screened front porch of a house with a couch, two large mirrors and a coat rack by a screen door. An extraordinary sheen surrounded the image and I could almost smell the new pine floor of the porch. I described the scene as I stepped slightly to my right, explaining I was moving to see my reflection more easily in one of the mirrors.

"That's my hat in front of you," said Sherry, one of the trainers. "And that's our newly renovated porch in Miami. That rack is where I always hang my hat."

I had never been to Sherry's home. But the more I answered her questions, the more accurately I described the front of her house. No one was able to explain it, and to this day it is my only ESP experience. The sensory-based blitz they put me through had somehow altered my neural wiring, allowing me to tap into another level of comprehension.

Inspired by my visions, Sherry and her husband hosted a workshop called "ESP or NLP?" a year later. I took part along with well-known psychics, but despite our efforts nobody created a spontaneous incident like mine.

After this experience I no longer believe ESP requires a "sixth sense." I think it's just a different way of connecting the five senses we already possess. My senses had never been more intensely tapped and cross-related than that day in Monterey.

I considered trying to replicate an ESP experience on my own. But in a way, composing *is* an ESP experience. I hear things that others don't. In fact, I also see and feel what I'm hearing, sometimes all three at once. I might even taste them, because I sometimes grimace as if they have a bitter flavor. It's not clairvoyance *per se*, but a clairvoyance of sound. Call it clairaudience. ❋

THEN I STOOD ON
MY HEAD

I THOUGHT I WAS A PRETTY GOOD SPEAKER UNTIL I GAVE A LUNCH talk at St. Michael's Hospital in Toronto. Asked to talk about NLP, I watched as doctors and nurses walked in and out, nibbled at their sandwiches and occasionally dozed off. I hoped most of them were tired from all-night shifts, but I wasn't sure. At the end of the day, I poured myself a generous scotch and swore to never let that happen again.

A few months later, I walked into a large classroom for a talk to the Ontario College of Physicians. Wearing a dark suit and tie—unnecessarily formal for the occasion—I assumed a rigid stance and spoke in a mechanical voice, pausing between words for robotic effect. "NLP is...the study...of...subjective behavior." (Pause) "NLP is also...the study of...objective behavior." (Pause) "So...you could say that... NLP is the study of...subjective...and objective...behavior."

I caught a few of their glances: "Oh no, an hour and a half of *this?*" I didn't relent. Droning on, I gradually undressed—loosening my tie, taking off my jacket, dropping my slacks—until I was naked except for a pair of black gym shorts. Then I stood on my head and twisted my body, somersaulting into a shoulder stand. I shifted to the other shoulder, somersaulted again and rolled around the floor. Finishing in a headstand, I recited one of my poems:

> *"Skyscrapers are trees of the city*
> *People are fallen leaves*
> *Changing color by economy*
> > *Humanities up two-thirds*
> > *Communications down*
> *I'll buy a hundred shares of AT&T*
> *If someone will please*
> > *Communicate with me"*

Still upside-down, I told them to close their eyes. They did. I quickly stood up and put on my clothes (an operation I had carefully practiced for speed), combed my hair, sat on a stool and said, "Open your eyes." I asked them to tell me what had just happened. The reports were astonishingly varied.

"You talked about nature."

"You did some acrobatics."

"You stood on your head with your suit on."

"You were completely naked."

I pointed to a person I knew was visually oriented—by the upward movement of his eyes—and he gave a pretty accurate account. Then I called on a more feeling type who recalled only a few details.

On the easel I drew the NLP eye-scan chart, showing how people's eye movements reveal whether they are thinking visually, auditorily or what is called in NLP "kinesthetically"—feeling related. (Eyes up: visual. Eyes sideways: auditory. Eyes down-left: internal dialogue. Eyes down-right: feeling.)

To demonstrate, I asked the kinesthetic grad student to sit up front and recount what I had done. I asked the audience to note that his eyes were in the down-right position while talking. When

I asked him to look up into the visual position and give his report again, he filled in the details he had forgotten before: me undressing, me on my head, me reciting poetry in my shorts.

A lively discussion followed as the doctors and students experimented with different eye positions to see how it affected their memory and learning. I took away my own memory of people engaged in new ideas, rather than staring at their sandwiches and dozing off. ✳

ENEMIES INTO ALLIES

ONE DAY AN 84-YEAR-OLD WOMAN NAMED FREDA TOLD ME SHE was inhabited by a demon who was trying to kill her. She had heard that I'd gotten rid of my demon and wanted me to exorcise hers too. I told her that she had it all wrong—my demon was creative, my best friend and ally.

"Well, mine isn't any kind of friend," she said. "I like to paint and write poetry, but he won't let me. He's just like my father."

I thought hypnosis might help, so with her agreement I put her into a trance. I agreed that she could record the session.

Once she fell under, I said I wanted to talk to her "demon." A strong masculine voice barked, "Well, I don't want to talk to you!"

I was stunned. This gentle elderly woman now seemed almost dangerous. I tried to compose myself. "I'd like to get to know you if I could. Perhaps you would be willing to let another part of Freda talk to me on your behalf?"

"You're very clever," the voice sneered.

"I don't mean to be clever, I just want to help her."

"I want to end this conversation—*now*."

Because she was wearing a pacemaker, I didn't want to push her and ended the trance. When she awoke she saw she had reflexively turned off her tape recorder. "He wouldn't let me record this," she said. "He never lets me do anything I want."

Stalemate. What could I do? After she left, I felt I had failed her. But days later she called and said, "I wrote a poem," and asked for another session.

This time, I suggested we meet at her home so we could be in her natural environment. On a whim, I took along a recording of the Mozart *Piano Sonata in F Major*. When I walked into her ornately decorated house—lace curtains, flowered upholstery, cabinets full of knick-knacks—I saw she also had a stereo. We made small talk until I suggested some exercises. I showed her several different ways of stepping—forward, left, right, backwards and diagonal. We stepped around the room in these various ways until she felt the rhythm of us moving together.

Then I put on the slow movement of the Mozart. She smiled and moved with great pleasure—then suddenly stopped and started crying. I asked what was wrong and she whimpered haltingly, "No one has ever done this with me before." I told her she did it very well and we continued dancing until the recording ran out.

I said, "Isn't it nice to know that you can do something creative without anybody stopping you?"

She phoned a few weeks later. "I've made two paintings and a magazine just agreed to publish some of my new poetry," she said. "I think my demon has become a new friend." ❋

"How Do I Stand it?"

My wife, Ulla, has struggled mightily at times to communicate with me and our son Neal. Both of us have a tendency to disappear into our creative fogs in the middle of a conversation. Here's one she captured verbatim.

* * *

The three of us were returning home from dinner in a Japanese restaurant, when I wanted to tell "the boys" about the charming new puppy on our block. It replaced a beautiful Collie that was a fixture in the neighborhood for many years. However, I didn't want to strain their minds by saying, as a normal person would: "The Collie on the block has died and the owner now has a very charming boxer that I met today for the first time." Instead, I gave one fact at a time and it went like this:

Ulla: Remember the Collie on the block?
Neal: No, what's a Collie?
U: It's a big dog, like Lassie.
Michael: What block?
U: Why, our block, of course.
M: Well, when you begin with "remember" I think right away of other blocks in the past.

U: Anyway, it was on our block and it died of old age. Now the girl's got a new puppy.

N: What girl?

U: The owner. She's the young painter who lives in the red house north of the parking lot.

M: You said girl. You mean woman.

N: Yes, that makes a big difference.

U: You know who I mean then?

N: No.

M: No.

U: But you knew the Collie.

N & M: No, we never saw the dog, did we?

U: How can you not have seen the dog? It paraded up and down the sidewalk for 10 years and was as big as a pony.

M: No, I swear I never saw it. What about it?

U: Well, it died. And while I was gardening out front today, the girl came by with the cutest puppy, a black boxer. So we were introduced for the first time.

M: To the woman, you mean?

U: No, to the puppy. It's a really great dog.

N: So now that we know this, what's the story?

U: That is the story. A well-known dog has died and a new dog now lives on our block.

M: You mean after this long explanation, that's the whole story?

U: Yes. I think it's fairly interesting. And it wouldn't need a long explanation under normal circumstances.

N: Boy, I'm really excited.

* * *

Let this be a warning: think again before hooking up with an artist, unless you're ready for conversations like this one. They could create problems, but fortunately in our family they usually end in laughter. ❋

GETTING RELIGION IN THE ARCTIC

I SPENT A MONTH IN THE CANADIAN ARCTIC WITH AN INUIT FAMILY in Pangnirtung, Baffin Island, in the spring of 1988. I wanted to get a feel for the great north and write music about it.

When the men invited me on a seal hunt, my host Rosie Aka-lukyuk told me how lucky I was: I would get to eat the liver of a seal when they caught one. She explained with enthusiasm that they would cut it out on the spot and I would eat this rare delicacy while they watched.

I had been raised Catholic, but around age 12 or 13 I became dis-illusioned and left the church for good. Now I found myself making a few promises to God and had no trouble praying again: "Please, Lord, don't let them catch a seal. I'll do anything you ask."

My one hope was that a seal might go unnoticed in this giant tundra. But I had read about Inuit eyesight—that they could spot the red slits of a white bird's eyes against the snow at 50 yards.

Then one of the hunters pointed into the distance. "See that tent?" I looked but saw nothing. One of them focused a pair of high-powered field glasses and handed them to me. Still I couldn't see it. "Keep looking," they said, adjusting my aim. Gradually a faint yellow speck began to appear in the distance, which I assumed was the tent. If they could see this, how could they miss a seal?

As the day went on, my prayers intensified. Once or twice my heart jumped as one of the hunters pointed to something amid the icebergs. But I guess God took pity on me because they never did find a seal. To this day, when I see liver on a menu I move on. ❋

GROUP THERAPY, INUIT STYLE

ALCOHOL IS FORBIDDEN BY LAW IN THE ARCTIC BECAUSE OF THE Inuit's congenital inability to handle booze. Hard drink affects them like LSD does the average Westerner, and they stop drinking only when the bottle is empty.

One day a friend of my host Enukie Akalukyuk smuggled a bottle of vodka into Pangnirtung. We didn't know about it until it was too late. Enukie secretly drank the whole bottle in an hour. I heard him ranting and thrashing wildly as two friends tried to subdue him. Neighbors ran over to help while Rosie wailed, worried sick about her husband.

After much struggle they calmed him down, poured coffee into him and got him to lie in bed. Through her tears, Rosie explained that Enukie was ranting about his sister, who had committed suicide about 10 years earlier—a tragedy he never got over and felt he could have prevented. His repressed guilt came to the surface like a tormenting demon.

The next day was quiet. About two dozen villagers, men and women of all ages, came over and sat on the floor. Enukie, now sober, sat at a table facing them. Those who could not fit inside stood quietly around the front porch. One by one the villagers spoke. I didn't understand the language of course, but Rosie whispered in my ear that they were telling stories about their own struggles with death, suicide and guilt. I felt the intent and emotion of each person as they gestured and raised their voices almost as if they were singing. Every so often the visitors would murmur in agreement as they listened.

A deep sense of communion pervaded the room. Every so often Enukie would wipe his tears away. This went on from dawn to dusk as food and drink was served.

The usual group therapy sessions we know depend on a leader. With Enukie there was no group leader. Nor was there any sense of criticism or judgment of Enukie's behavior. It was a beautiful and poignant experience.

Enukie looked refreshed the following day. He actually appeared younger. He moved energetically and had a relaxed smile. I told Rosie I thought Enukie's alcoholic binge might have benefitted him, thanks to their friends and neighbors. "Yes, it was good," she said. "He got it all out." ❋

THE WRONG CHURCH

I THINK MY MOTHER'S NATURAL SKEPTICISM MADE ME CRITICAL OF religion. Her Irish father told her there was only one church—Catholic, of course. But my mother, who was one of 18 children, had an independent streak.

One Sunday she went to a Protestant church with a friend. When she came home, her father confronted her angrily, saying her Catholic friends had been looking for her.

"I did go to church, with Evelyn."

"But Evelyn goes to the wrong church," he said.

"But you said there was only one church, so how could I have gone to the wrong one?"

She said he never discussed religion with her again. ❧

A LESSON FROM
THE IRISH SEA

HOW MANY TIMES HAVE I BEEN ASKED WHY I CREATE MUSIC? My answers vary—self-expression, spiritual exploration, reflecting on the age we live in. Classical composers were known to write, "To the glory of God" on scores. But I was never fully satisfied with such answers. Not that they were untrue, just incomplete.

One day I heard an answer that rang true. I was in Dublin visiting the James Joyce Tower. When I walked down the road I saw the Forty-Foot, an inlet where people swim in the Irish Sea year-round. At that time, it was still for men only and they swam nude.

Since no swimsuit was required, I decided to give it a try. I was warned the water was about 11 Celsius, or 51 Fahrenheit—in other words, extremely cold! But I loved to swim and had braved frigid water before.

The area was all natural rock abutting the deeply green ocean. The only man-made thing was a ladder descending into the deep. So I took off my clothes and climbed down for a quick dip. I dipped in and out quickly to insulate my body and then braved a full swim. I crawl-stroked a few icy yards in a small circle. The water was so cold that I felt like a leather band was tightening around my forehead. I stayed in for only a minute and scrambled out. I'd had enough.

As I was drying myself with my T-shirt, a tall, well-muscled man of about 80 took off his clothes, dove in and swam leisurely on his back as if he were in the Bahamas. I watched him go out about a hundred yards, swim around and freestyle his way back. As he climbed out, I said, "You look like you've done this before."

He answered in his Irish brogue, "Ah, your first time is it? Well, it's like poverty—all in what you're used to." He dried himself with a towel. "So what do you do?"

"I'm a composer," I said. "Symphonies, that sort of thing."

"Ahhh, love-ly, love-ly, love-ly." He threw his head back and laughed in delight. "For most of us life is so mundaaa-ne."

For the first time I heard a satisfactory answer to why I compose: it is never boring. Of all the things I've done in my life I can't think of one as endlessly challenging. Aggravating, puzzling, frustrating, enervating, yes—but never mundane.

I heard it straight from the Irish Sea. ❊

COMMUNICATING BY ICEBERG

MY EXTRASENSORY EXPERIENCE IN MONTEREY WASN'T ACTUALLY MY only brush with ESP. After staying in the Arctic, I wrote a piece for organ and orchestra called *Snow Walker*. It included a section called "Ice and Light," written to evoke the image of an iceberg reflecting the light of the sun, the ever-changing colors as it slowly floats by during spring thaw.

I was concentrating strongly on writing the movement in my Toronto studio, when my wife told me to pick up the phone— unusual for her because she rarely interrupts my work.

"It's Rosie from Pangnirtung," she said.

I hadn't made contact with Rosie and Enukie since leaving the Arctic three years before. They weren't the letter-writing kind and I had never seen them use a telephone. I'd sent a thank-you letter, but never heard back.

"Hi, Rosie? Are you visiting Toronto?" I asked.

"No," she said. "Enukie and I were just sitting outside in the sun, watching this big iceberg float by with all the colors shining on it, and I said to him, 'Let's call Michael.'"

We chatted for a few minutes and I never heard from them again. ❧

Tired Tongue in Bali

I spent two summers in Bali as part of a team teaching NLP to entrepreneurs from around the world. Balinese culture was like another world; people here appeared so noncompetitive, happy the way they were. Their language has no word for art, yet everyone we met spent their afternoons creating—painting, playing music, dancing, or designing something beautiful.

On our days off, we tried to learn the customs of people living in and around Ubud. A group went to visit Cok Roi, a renowned healer in the village of Puri Nagari. His "clinic" was a raised platform with a thatched roof. Ageless in appearance, Roi had lines of wisdom around the eyes, but he was slim and smooth-skinned like a teenager.

He received us sitting on a straw mat with his pet owl and several villagers looking on. One by one we stepped up on his wooden perch to let him measure our health. He vigorously kneaded the top of each person's head with his steely fingers to form a diagnosis.

When he probed my head, he suddenly pressed hard on one spot and pain shot through my skull. "Ah-hah!" he said. Then he pressed a chopstick between the third and fourth toe of my left foot. I jumped back in pain.

"Ow!"

"Yes, you have tired tongue!"

He advised me to rest and not think or talk for at least two days. His advice made sense. I had just finished several weeks of intense planning and teaching NLP to 75 international entrepreneurs. It was quite a contrast to my composing life.

The healer, or balian, showed me one of his favorite paintings to help me cure my tired mind and tongue. It depicted a man sitting in a lotus position with a light shining through his head from above, straight down to his groin. The five "chakras" were brightly illuminated along the path of the powerful beam. The man's tongue was stretched out of his mouth to his right side to allow a free pathway for the light to shine through the body.

To this day I think of that painting when I'm tired from too much dialogue, internal or external. Sure enough, my furious chatter quickly quiets down as I take deep breaths and relax my tongue. ❋

MY DECOMPOSING PANTS

BEETHOVEN ONCE TOLD A COMPOSITION STUDENT TO PUT A TABLE beside his keyboard to facilitate inspiration. So as a young composer, I put a slanted drawing table beside my piano. Later I did Beethoven one better and placed a second drawing table on my other side. Needing a flat surface for my tea mug and various papers, I eventually fit a regular table behind me. Now I was surrounded. My work surfaces gave me a kind of home within a home.

That enclosure is still an infallible creative anchor. Even if I'm fatigued or distracted and don't feel like composing, my creative juices flow when I enter that little circle of tables. I make it a point to only write music there—never letters or articles or books—and keep the surfaces clear of anything but drafts of new pieces. I have recreated that setup everywhere I've lived—New York, Copenhagen, London, Toronto—and it works every time. I'm sure I could compose in a subway station at rush hour if I had my keyboard and tables.

Clothing can also anchor me. A favorite shirt, sweater or slippers can trigger creative ideas if I wear them long enough while composing. I usually wear a bathrobe over my clothes to keep warm in my cool studio. Some neighbors actually thought I never worked because I was dressed as if I was just getting out of bed.

When I told violist Rivka Golani she owed me a bathrobe for the one I wore out writing her *Chaconne*, she came to my door and threw a red terry cloth bathrobe in my face. I wore it only for composing, especially when my mood was fiery.

My wife is still disturbed that I like to wear the same pants until I finish a piece. I call them my composing pants; she calls them my decomposing pants. One day when I had just finished an eight-month project—*Crossworlds* for flutist Marina Piccinini, pianist Andreas Haefliger and orchestra—she snatched my pants, carried them to the back yard and burned them. A sad moment, because I thought there were still some good notes left in those pants. ❃

"You Oughta Be on Facebook"

WHEN A YOUNG FRIEND TOLD ME, "HEY, MICHAEL, YOU OUGHTA be on Facebook," I recoiled. I have always preferred real human contact to computer screens.

But she insisted on showing me how it works. I was especially intrigued by Facebook groups. With the creativity projects I had devised for children, I thought this might be a way to push for new ideas in music education. So I created a group called "Dusting off Music Educators," inviting people to talk about their favorite music teachers.

Responses rolled in. One, from a high school band director in Nova Scotia, invited me to write a new piece with his students and perform it—all in four days. I suggested we go a step further and let his students write and conduct their own music.

So I flew to Middleton, Nova Scotia, and taught Richard Bennett and his Middleton High School Band students about graphic notation. I showed them how graphics—wavy lines, straight lines, dots and curlicues—can be interpreted as pitches and rhythms. They can be used to create music without extensive composition training.

The students started by writing a graphic piece together, singing out their ideas as they took turns drawing on the blackboard.

After singing and conducting the piece several ways, they each wrote a graphic piece on their own, taping them on the blackboard for everyone to sing. Those who wanted to compose for our concert then spent the next three days writing graphic pieces with my help.

On the evening of the fourth day, seven student composers conducted their own music for a good-sized audience of parents and other Middletonians. The students talked about their pieces and displayed their graphic notation on overhead projectors. One young composer conducted her piece with dance movements, cueing entrances by pointing, waving her arms, swooping her body around, and finishing with a dramatic leap as she gave her last cue and disappeared behind a tuba player. At the end of the concert, the audience cheered on their feet.

For months after, messages from students kept popping into my Facebook page. A fine arts consultant for the Nova Scotia Department of Education, Ardith Haley—who attended part of our workshop—wrote that she decided to team up with Richard to lobby for graphic notation in the Nova Scotia junior high schools.

A group of music teachers in Halifax soon invited Richard to show them graphic notation. Many admitted they had avoided teaching composition because they found it intimidating. With graphic notation, they said, they felt confident enough to turn students into composers.

I now have greater respect for electronic helpers like Facebook—though I still don't carry a cell phone. ✳

POST-HUMOROUS WORKS

I'M FASCINATED BY THE FACT THAT A COMPOSER'S VALUE USUALLY increases from the grave—far more than the value given to living composers.

I've rarely heard of a composer who was satisfied with a payment for a work, but even mediocre composers can generate good money posthumously. Take a relatively insignificant composer like the Russian Vassili Kalinnikov. When Sergei Rachmaninoff took Kalinnikov's music to a publisher to obtain funds for the deceased composer's widow, the publisher said, "Don't imagine that I pay this tremendous sum without a definite reason: I pay it because the death of the composer has multiplied the value of his works by ten." It was a smooth way of telling Rachmaninoff not to expect the same deal.

It is still uncouth for a composer to show interest in money. A composer is supposed to be a kind of secular priest whose rewards are artistic and spiritual, yet we must pay our way through life like everyone else. According to the American Music Center, only 10% of composers make their living from writing music—so most composers aim for university tenure.

Beethoven expressed frustration about this in a letter to Franz Anton Hoffmeister in 1801: "There should be a single arts exchange in the world to which the artist would simply send his works and be

given in return as much as he needs. As it is, one has to be half mer-
chant on top of everything else, and how badly one goes about it."
Of course, Beethoven's work is now generating a lot of money. The
trouble is he's no longer around to collect it.

So what, you might ask, is the solution? Let me offer a novel one:
that the composer be alive and dead at the same time. Impossible?
Consider this.

Let's say you're a composer and want to reap the benefits of
your own death—while remaining alive. The first thing you'd do
is disappear, leaving behind tantalizing clues to stimulate people's
imaginations, like a message scrawled on a torn piece of your latest manuscript saying, "My life is a failure." The last few bars could
be written in a shaky hand trailing off the edge of the page. Your
photo would appear in the press, with a caption like: "Has anyone
seen this person?" The evening news—well, the local news—would
show search parties scanning wooded areas.

The aura of mystery surrounding your name would ignite gossip
in the music world. With stories concluding that you were "missing
and presumed dead," orchestras and opera companies would begin
to show interest in the works of this "much-neglected composer"—
especially works as yet unperformed. A world premiere by a dead
composer would be a real coup.

Meanwhile you would visit a cemetery in a distant town and
scribble down a few names from gravestones. With any luck, you
could steal an identity by applying for a "lost" birth certificate,
which authorities can grant by mail. New name in hand, you could
apply for credit cards to tide you over until royalties started rolling
in. Your checks would be mailed to a relative named in your will—
a coconspirator who always thought you were misunderstood and
would write money orders to your new name.

Then you would rent a nice quiet apartment and write as many
posthumous works as possible, which you could plant at strategic

points around the country to be "discovered." You might even hide intriguing bits of information about yourself to be discovered by academics—like a packet of unmailed letters to a mysterious unnamed lover, revealing fascinating romantic tidbits or personal habits. Stories about your unrequited love would appear in the media.

When your success begins to peak, you would play your trump card: a return to life! Any composer can die, but how many have come back from the dead?

Fame would be yours forever. News magazines would splash our face across covers. Talk shows would hound you for appearances. Commissions and guest conducting offers would flood in at high fees. Someone might sue you for fraud, but you'd get a good lawyer—now affordable—and argue that it was a victimless crime. Your disappearance and loss of contact with friends and loved ones could simply be attributed to your "lack of contact with reality"—a typical state for a composer. At worst, you might pay a fine or serve a short sentence, which would generate even more publicity about abused artists.

So to my friends, I say, "Don't be too quick to grieve when I die. I might just be basking on a beach in the Bahamas between visits to my broker." ❈

APPENDIX

Selected Recordings of Michael Colgrass

Arctic Dreams

For large wind ensemble. *A tone poem about life in the Arctic, with musical depictions of ice floating in the sun, the aurora borealis, polar nights, Inuit throat-singing, the spring hunt and drum dancing.*

Arctic Dreams. Battisti, Frank, conductor. New England Conservatory Wind Ensemble and Chorus. Centaur Records, CRC 2288.

Chaconne

For viola and orchestra. *A theme and 23 variations exploring the viola in a variety of concertante settings traversing 300 years of musical styles.*

Chaconne. Davis, Andrew, conductor. On *Chaconne.* The Toronto Symphony Orchestra. Rivka Golani, soloist. CBC Records 2-5087.

Concertmasters

For three violins and orchestra. *Three violins portrayed like actors in a play, going through a series of dialogues and confrontations, sometimes romantic, often atonal, based on an original baroque theme.*

Concertmasters. Akiyama, Kazuyoshi, conductor. On *The American Symphony Orchestra*. Vox 5158.

Déjà vu

For percussion quartet and orchestra. *Four percussionists playing four separate solos, often in separate tempi, while exploring percussion colors in various musical styles.*

Déjà vu. Slatkin, Leonard, conductor. On *World Premiere Recordings*. The Saint Louis Symphony Orchestra. New World Records NW 318.

Déjà vu

For four percussionists and wind ensemble.

Déjà vu. Corporan, Eugene, conductor. On *Deja View*. North Texas Wind Symphony. KLAVIER KCD-11091.

Dream Dancer

For alto saxophone and wind ensemble. *A fantasy about an alto saxophone player who feels attracted to Mideastern, Asian and American cultures all at once, and struggles to reconcile them into one music.*

Dream Dancer. Gomes, Tony, conductor. On *Northern Winds*. Toronto Wind Orchestra. Wallace Hallady, alto saxophone. NAXOS/Wind Band Classics 8.572248.

———. Peltz, Charles, conductor. On *Déjà vu*. New England Conservatory Wind Ensemble, Kenneth Radnofsky, soloist. Albany Record MODE 125.

_____. Green, Gary, conductor. University of Miami Wind Ensemble. Lynn Klock, alto saxophone. Albany Records, 525.

Hammer & Bow

For violin and marimba. *A duet combining a variety of violin and marimba effects to reflect the mysterious and unpredictable mood changes of two people in a close relationship.*

Hammer & Bow. On *Suite Fantaisie.* Jacques Israelievitch, violin, Michael Israelievitch, marimba. Fleur de son Classics FDS 57941.

Light Spirit

For flute, viola, guitar and two percussion players. *A light and jazzy atonal piece for flute, viola, guitar and two percussion.*

Light Spirit. Comet, Catherine, conductor. On *World Premiere Recordings.* The Saint Louis Symphony Players. New World Records NW 318.

Snow Walker

The Snow Walker is the Inuit spirit that escorts human beings in their transition from the earth to the stars.

Snow Walker. Kalmar, Carlos, conductor. On *American Works for Organ and Orchestra.* Grant Park Orchestra. David Schrader, organ. Cedille Records CDR 90000 0 063.

Urban Requiem

A large-scale work where soloists and accompanying ensemble (average-size symphony orchestra without strings broken up into various "neighborhoods") interact while expressing the diversity, humor and tragedy inherent in our cities.

Urban Requiem. Kirchoff, Craig, conductor. On *White Heat Into Blue Dawn.* University of Minnesota Wind Ensemble. Innova Records CD 517.

_____. Green, Gary, conductor. On *New Music for Winds and Percussion*. University of Miami Wind Ensemble. Albany Records Troy 212.

Variations for Four Drums and Viola

A virtuoso duet introducing tuned drums, which has become a repertory piece for violists.

Variations for Four Drums and Viola. On *Rivka Golani*. Rivka Golani, violist. Ryan Scott, percussionist. Centrediscs CMC CD 5798.

_____. On *The Elegant Viola*. Yizhak Schotten, violist. Frank Epstein, percussionist. Crystal Records CD 837.

Winds of Nagual: A Musical Fable on the Writings of Carlos Castaneda

For wind ensemble. *A tone poem based on the books of Carlos Castaneda about his adventures with the Yaqui Indian sorcerer don Juan.*

Winds of Nagual: A Musical Fable on the Writings of Carlos Castaneda. Battisti, Frank, conductor. On *Live from Jordan Hall*. New England Conservatory of Music Wind Ensemble. Albany Records TROY 560.

_____. Thompson, Mallory, conductor. On *Winds of Nagual*. Northwestern University Symphonic Wind Ensemble. Summit Records DCD-313.

_____. Mikkelson, Russel, conductor. On *Wind Band Classics*. Ohio State University Wind Ensemble. Naxos/Wind Band Classics 8.570244.

Scores by Michael Colgrass are available from Carl Fischer LLC, Symphonic music Division, 65 Bleeker Street, New York, NY 10012. For rental library, e-mail info@presser.com.

Book by Michael Colgrass

My Lessons with Kumi: How I Learned to Perform with Confidence. A narrative instruction book on performance preparation.

Real People Press, 2000.

Available through Realpeoplepress.com or Amazon.com.